EVERLASTING

Peaks, Valleys, and Grace in the Psalms

CHRISTINA HERGENRADER

CONCORDIA PUBLISHING HOUSE · SAINT LOUIS

DEDICATION

For Barb Tanz
Thank you for twenty years of love, support, and listening.
You are an everlasting model of God's love.

Published by Concordia Publishing House
3558 S. Jefferson Ave., St. Louis, MO 63118-3968
1-800-325-3040 · cph.org

Manufactured in the United States of America.

1 2 3 4 5 6 7 8 9 10 34 33 32 31 30 29 28 27 26 25

The Psalms are deeply personal, and in this book, Christina encourages us to relish their vivid imagery, see the presence of Jesus, and be assured of God's provision and love. Her vulnerable and genuine storytelling paired with solid scriptural truths and insight encouraged me to read the Psalms out loud and to use them as prayers for my own heart cries and joyful praises. From beginning to end, this book will be a blessing.

—Eden Keefe, president of Lutheran Women in Mission, 2023–27

Everlasting is an emotional guidebook to the Psalms. In addition to providing important historical and literary information, Christina Hergenrader guides readers through this book of the Bible, highlighting various emotions. Do you feel helpless? Stay in Psalm 116 for a while. Confused? Try Psalm 56. Joyful? Park in Psalm 3. *Everlasting* provides a map through the beloved book of Psalms as you navigate the messy emotions of life.

—Sharla Fritz, author of *Measured by Grace: How God Defines Success* and *Waiting: A Bible Study on Patience, Hope, and Trust*

Christina does an incredible job of showing the beauty of the Psalms and expressing our deepest emotions before God. Whether in sorrow, joy, fear, or praise, the Psalms reassure us that we are never alone. Christina reminds us to bring our burdens before the Lord, knowing He hears and comforts us in every season. If you seek peace, hope, or simply a place to rest your weary heart, Psalms is a wellspring of divine comfort and unwavering truth. This is a book that I can already see myself giving to so many of my loved ones as they walk through those hard moments.

—Faith Doerr, author of *God's Encouraging Word: True Comforts When Worldly Advice Fails*

Are you looking for honesty, connection, and encouragement in the struggles and celebrations of life? In this lovely book, author Christina Hergenrader weaves real-life stories with God's care for us today, communicated through the book of Psalms. She connects our humanity—our emotions, experiences, ups and downs—to its ancient, heartfelt words. We are inspired, uplifted, and reminded of His enduring love!

—Martha Van Buskirk, speaker and author of *Ordinary Lives Extraordinary Grace: God's Purpose in Your Every Day*

In a world that often urges us to push through feelings, *Everlasting* encourages us to acknowledge their temporary yet significant importance while reflecting on how Jesus experienced them and walks with us through our own. Through vulnerable storytelling, practical guides, and prayer prompts, Christina reminds us that the Psalms are not just words on a page but emotion-filled messages that speak directly to our hearts. *Everlasting* is a beautiful read, whether reflected on with close friends, studied in a small group, or enjoyed alone with a cup of coffee.

—Elizabeth Cattau, advancement officer, Lutheran South Academy, Houston, Texas

Christina's writing has always resonated with me, and this book is no exception. Her captivating stories are filled with truth, love, humor, and joy. Her heartfelt descriptions of the Psalms make it easier for me to understand and connect to my emotions. She offers questions that make me stop and ponder, which causes me to grow even closer to the Lord. This book will be extremely powerful on its own but might make a bigger impact if studied with a small group of like-minded people you can share honestly with.

—Sara Leimkuehler, kindergarten teacher, Deep Waters Academy, Houston, Texas

Christina Hergenrader's *Everlasting: Peaks, Valleys, and Grace in the Psalms* is like having coffee with a wise friend who totally gets it. She brilliantly connects ancient psalms to our messy, modern lives with stories that'll make you laugh, nod in recognition, and occasionally tear up. Her relational style cuts through the noise, offering genuine insight without the churchy jargon. Whether you're feeling anxious, lost, or hopeful, Christina's warm wisdom reminds us we're never alone—God's love is everlasting through every emotion we face.

—Michelle Thompson, MA, MS, PCC, senior director, Townsend Institute at Concordia University Irvine

Christina shares story after story of present-day needs and human emotions alongside the goodness and faithfulness of God revealed by these psalms of old. Together they paint a beautiful picture of what it is to be human, to have a companion and champion who is constant in life's ups and downs, and to be so dearly loved.

—Jamie Wiechman, cofounder of Breathe Life Ministries

TABLE OF CONTENTS

> Come and see what God has done:
> He is awesome in His deeds.
> Psalm 66:5

> The Psalter is the book of all saints; and everyone, in whatever situation he may be, finds in that situation psalms and words that fit his case, that suit him as if they were put there just for his sake.
> – Martin Luther

Welcome to *Everlasting: Peaks, Valleys, and Grace in the Psalms*

Hi, friend!

Thanks so much for picking up this book. It's been a journey to write it.

Over the past three years, I've been working on these stories from my life, weaving them together with the Psalms. Honestly, I didn't always know where this project was headed. I just kept writing, hoping that somehow the threads would come together into something meaningful.

Psalms has always been one of my favorite books of the Bible, but this time, during this project, I was reading the verses with new eyes. Now that I'm in the middle of my life, the words of these psalms hit me differently. I felt seen—this is exactly what life feels like. Epic highs of seeing God's work in my life and crushing lows of loss and unbelievable pain. Life had introduced me to a new range of emotions, and the laments and praises in the Psalms felt richer than before.

I realized I wanted to feel something again—really feel it. Maybe you know what I mean. We can get so caught up in gathering information, staying busy, and managing the day-to-day that we barely notice we've stopped feeling much of anything. It's like our emotions get buried under a pile of tasks and expectations. I began looking to the Psalms to stir something in me, to help me reconnect with emotions I tucked away.

But, even then, I wasn't quite sure where this was leading.

In the middle of all that uncertainty, I took a detour (middle age is like this, right?). I enrolled in a two-year executive coaching program through Concordia University Irvine in California. It was a time of deep learning about how we process emotions, how they connect us and make life richer, and how they remind us of our shared human frailty.

That experience opened my eyes in so many ways, but even with that insight, something still felt incomplete. I kept asking myself these questions: Why do our emotions matter? Why were the psalmists so comfortable writing about how they felt, but so many of us today are not? As Christians, what do we do with our anger, our shame, our regret?

Here's what I learned: Emotions matter. They matter to God, and they matter in our lives. We're created to feel, to fully experience what is in our hearts. Emotions are as much a part of us as our lungs and brains are. The Psalms show us this—how to praise in the peaks and lament in the valleys.

So, why do we so often avoid our feelings? Are we afraid that feeling ashamed or angry means we don't trust God, that we aren't Christian enough?

Then one day, everything clicked. I was reading Psalm 90 and verse 2 stopped me: "Before the mountains were brought forth, or ever You had formed the earth and the world, from everlasting to everlasting You are God."

That's the message. Whether you're at the peak of joy or walking through a valley of pain, God's love remains the same. His grace lasts. This is the steadying force we cling to. From the very beginning of creation to the moment you are reading this, through all of eternity, God's love remains steady, unchanging, and everlasting.

This is the truth the psalmists clung to and the reminder we need right now. Kingdoms crumble, pain paralyzes us, joy inspires us, everything we think we know changes—except God's everlasting love for us.

In the peaks and valleys, feelings are important, but they're temporary. We can fully feel the grief, the anger, the awe, the helplessness that are part of life. Why? Because all of it points us to God's everlasting love.

This is why the words in Psalms are so important. These aren't just any words—they're God's words for our emotions, His way of meeting us exactly where we are. In the Psalms, God gives us language for every feeling, reminding us that our emotions are part of being human.

It's so good to feel deeply, to be honest about our struggles, to know that each emotion we feel is an expression of being fully alive. Our emotions pass like waves, but God's love remains steady, anchoring us to Him no matter how we feel or what we face.

So, as we explore these psalms together, I invite you to bring your whole self. Remember both your mountaintop moments and your dark valleys. Be vulnerable. Let yourself feel these emotions, then reflect on your own story. And be honest with God. Secure in His love, you can embrace your emotions, knowing this is healthy.

But let's also remember that His love is what holds us together.

Through every high and low, every moment of joy and struggle, you are never alone. God's love is here, steady and true, ready to nourish your heart and fill you with hope.

Love,
Christina

How to Use *Everlasting*

Because Your steadfast love is better than life,
my lips will praise You.
Psalm 63:3

1. Learn about the psalm type.

Everlasting is divided into five sections named after the five types of psalms: Thanksgiving, Wisdom, Lament, Praise, and Messianic. At the start of each section, read about the type of psalm and look for those characteristics in the stories and psalms that follow.

If you're reading this book with a group, you can study one type of psalm each week.

2. Read the psalm.

Take your time. Read the psalm slowly, savoring the words and images. Let the psalm writer's emotions and vivid language sink in. Feel free to read it more than once, letting it resonate deeply.

3. Find yourself in the story.

As you read the story that accompanies the psalm, think of your own story. What about this experience feels familiar? What have you gone through that echoes the emotions in the psalm?

4. Feel your emotions.

Let yourself truly feel—whether it's sorrow, joy, gratitude, or awe. Notice how your body reacts. Where do you feel tension or release? Take deep breaths and be present with whatever comes up. Emotions are part of being human, and it's okay to experience them fully.

5. Really understand the psalm.

Ask yourself: What does this psalm teach me about life, human nature, or God? How does this connect me to generations of believers who've experienced similar feelings? How do these emotions help me understand God's love?

6. Embrace God's everlasting love.

No matter what emotions you feel, remember they're temporary. God's love is the anchor that holds steady through everything. My hope and my prayer are that the twenty-five psalms discussed in *Everlasting* leave you with a deeper understanding that you are held by God.

7. See Jesus in these words.

These psalms are saturated with the presence of Jesus. They give words to His own prayers, His cries of anguish, and His songs of joy. As we read them, we see glimpses of the grace, peace, and forgiveness that Jesus came to fulfill. He is the Good Shepherd of Psalm 23, the rejected Cornerstone of Psalm 118, and the Suffering Servant of Psalm 22. And He is the source of every comfort, every cry for mercy, and every celebration of salvation in these sacred songs. The more we read the psalms and take them to heart, the more we see Jesus woven into every word, drawing us deeper into His love.

8. Use the discussion questions.

Whether you're journaling alone or discussing with a group, the questions are here to help you apply the psalm's message to your life. Dive in, share your thoughts, and explore how God's Word speaks to you.

9. End in prayer.

You can use the prayer I've provided or speak from your heart. Thank God for His unchanging love, for meeting you in every emotion, every failure, every blessing. He is with you. And His love lasts forever.

JOIN OTHERS ON YOUR PSALMS JOURNEY

Everlasting works beautifully as a personal study or as a group study. Consider adding an accountability partner or forming a small group to walk through these psalms together. When you meet, share how these ancient songs speak into your life today. Let the conversations deepen your connections with God and with one another. One of God's greatest gifts is the community He's given you to help you experience His love more fully.

Thanksgiving Psalms

It is good to give thanks to the LORD, to sing praises to Your name, O Most High. Psalm 92:1

The Thanksgiving Psalms help you see life differently. They don't ignore your struggles or gloss over your joys but show how God's faithfulness holds everything together. As we've all discovered, life is far from flat—it's full of highs that take your breath away and lows that feel so, so dark. Gratitude points you back to God's steady presence.

As you read these psalms, take a moment to notice God's grace in your life. Where do you see His care in the beauty of nature? How does He provide for you and for the earth? How is He answering your prayers? Instead of focusing on struggles, focus on how God is with you, working even in the hardest or the smallest parts.

Meditate on these psalms and let them awaken a sense of wonder at everything God gives you. The most profound blessing they reveal is the unchanging love of your Savior. As you bring your emotions to the Lord—joys and sorrows alike—see His grace covering every aspect of your life. Thanksgiving is powerful. It shifts your focus from what's lacking to what God provides. It relieves stress and fills your heart with joy.

Make this ancient practice of praying the psalms a part of your faith journey. Use the Thanksgiving Psalms as a new lens to see your life through God's faithfulness. Every morning, let this practice remind you to be grateful in all things, trusting that God's blessings are present even in your ordinary moments.

Pleas for Mercy (Psalm 116)

Psalm 116 shows how thanksgiving rises from helplessness. The psalmist has walked through the valley and thanks God for His rescue: "I love the LORD, because He has heard my voice and my pleas for mercy" (v. 1). You and I feel this weakness because we've been there too. Yet, even in darkness, God's love breaks through: "For You have delivered my soul from death, my eyes from tears, my feet from stumbling" (v. 8). The gratitude here is real and raw, showing God's constant care.

For You Are with Me (Psalm 23)

Psalm 23 shifts us into a quiet, steady trust in our Shepherd's care. Life's path will have shadows of sin and doubt, but God walks with us: "Even though I walk through the valley of the shadow of death, I will fear no evil, for You are with me" (v. 4). The gratitude comes from knowing we never face hardship alone. We walk through the valley of the shadow of death to the greener pastures of heaven because of Jesus. David's response to God's care is overwhelming thanksgiving, and we join him in resting in God's love.

Awesome Deeds (Psalm 65)

Psalm 65 takes our gratitude to a place of awe: "By awesome deeds You answer us with righteousness, O God of our salvation" (v. 5). This psalm lifts our eyes to see God's care over all creation. Verse 6 reminds us of God's strength: "the one who by His strength established the mountains." God's gifts are awe inspiring, especially His gift of Jesus and the forgiveness of our sins (see v. 3).

Near to the Brokenhearted (Psalm 34)

Psalm 34 brings us back to our personal brokenness: "I sought the LORD, and He answered me and delivered me from all my fears" (v. 4). It includes this comforting truth: "The LORD is near to the brokenhearted and saves the crushed in spirit" (v. 18). We're grateful because God is here, holding us together when we feel like we're falling apart.

Bringing It All Together

The Thanksgiving Psalms invite us into a personal encounter with God's provision, teaching gratitude in everything. Whether you're celebrating or struggling, they show how to see God's hand in every moment. Thanksgiving threads through every season and emotion, holding everything together with His love.

Write Your Own Thanksgiving Psalm

A Thanksgiving Psalm is a prayer, a song, and a meditation to reflect on your life, emotions, and even your struggles. It helps you notice God's love and work, even in hard times. Grab a pen and write your own Thanksgiving Psalm, expressing gratitude for all He's done for you.

1. Start from a place of gratitude.

Where do you see God right now? Where have you seen His love, His care, His awesome power today? How has He surprised you with a way through your struggles? What is unbelievably beautiful in your life right now? Start with a list, and then let your heart overflow.

2. Create with vivid imagery.

As you create your psalm, use language that paints a picture. What do God's blessings feel or look like to you? Close your eyes and see what snapshot captures what God has done for you. Doodle a picture. Don't worry about using the perfect words; write what you see.

3. Get personal; be specific.

Dig into the details of your past. Remember God's small moments of grace: the day He helped you find your footing when you felt unhinged or how He has walked alongside you when you felt alone or terrified. Thanksgiving is for the everyday mercies. Let the personal details of your story shine in your psalm, just like David did.

4. Ground it in who God is.

Thanksgiving Psalms are rooted in who God is. As you write, reflect on His character—His steady love, His unshakable faithfulness, His patience with you. Point your psalm to these eternal qualities.

5. Remember you're part of a bigger story.

Your Thanksgiving Psalm isn't just about this particular day or season of your life. It connects you to the bigger picture, the larger arc of God's work throughout all of your life. The psalmists praised God for His faithfulness across generations. As you write, let your love for Jesus inspire your praise. Every blessing is a glimpse of His greater work in you and through you.

1. HELPLESS

Missing on an '80s Camping Trip

For Dad, who is never afraid to admit his weakness.

Psalm 116

1 I love the LORD, because He has heard
my voice and my pleas for mercy.
2 Because He inclined His ear to me,
therefore I will call on Him as long as I live.
3 The snares of death encompassed me;
the pangs of Sheol laid hold on me;
I suffered distress and anguish.
4 Then I called on the name of the LORD:
"O LORD, I pray, deliver my soul!"

5 Gracious is the LORD, and righteous;
our God is merciful.
6 The LORD preserves the simple;
when I was brought low, He saved me.
7 Return, O my soul, to your rest;
for the LORD has dealt bountifully with you.

8 For You have delivered my soul from death,
my eyes from tears,
my feet from stumbling;
9 I will walk before the LORD
in the land of the living.

10 I believed, even when I spoke:
"I am greatly afflicted";
11 I said in my alarm,
"All mankind are liars."

12 What shall I render to the LORD
for all His benefits to me?
13 I will lift up the cup of salvation
and call on the name of the LORD,
14 I will pay my vows to the LORD
in the presence of all His people.

15 Precious in the sight of the LORD
is the death of His saints.
16 O LORD, I am Your servant;
I am Your servant, the son of Your maidservant.
You have loosed my bonds.
17 I will offer to You the sacrifice of thanksgiving
and call on the name of the LORD.
18 I will pay my vows to the LORD
in the presence of all His people,
19 in the courts of the house of the LORD,
in your midst, O Jerusalem.
Praise the LORD!

Camping in the eighties? Totally different from today.

My parents were teachers, and when I was growing up, we could only afford vacations to Texas state parks. During the summers, we gathered with friends from church for epic camping trips. These vacations included sleeping in old tents, fishing in mossy lakes, and hiking miles of trails.

We didn't have today's space-age coolers or energy drinks. We had a musty canvas tent, an ancient Coleman stove, and plenty of unscheduled time. A gift of the eighties is all the free time we took for granted.

We all loved these trips. We constructed a tent village with six other families and then spent our days floating in the lake, playing horseshoes, and reading. When it got dark, we circled the fire for hot dogs and stories. At bedtime, we stumbled through the dark woods to the cinder block bathrooms and killed the spiders scurrying from the light before we took freezing showers. We sneezed all night in our muggy tents that smelled like mold.

How weird to feel so safe away from home, zipped into a black cocoon. Security and comfort cloaked all around us. Except that one terrifying memory—our infamous Eight-Mile Hike. It was a nightmare.

When nine of us elementary-age kids took off for a day-long hike, we just marched away from the campsite. Our parents didn't seem to care much. Of course, we didn't have cell phones. We also didn't have permission.

Three bold boys—the Purcell brothers—led the other six of us away from our tent village. I was seven years old, the youngest and the only girl. I would soon learn that I didn't belong with them.

As we hiked down the wide, dusty trail, the rambunctious boys jostled to be first. Now I realize that Dr Pepper and emerging testosterone fueled their competition, but then I thought they were cool. As we traveled farther down the narrowing trail, I felt an increasing danger. They were already hiking too fast for me. I knew I should turn around. But I didn't want them to call me a chicken.

After about a mile, my mouth was dry and I had to pee. Two unfortunate—and opposite—problems that made me feel helpless. My thick glasses slid down my nose, and sweat plastered my thin blonde hair to my neck.

Our leader, John, scared me. A fifth-grader, he cussed and told stories about feeding mice to his python, Luci. He had seen *The Exorcist* a dozen times and had read all Stephen King's books. He hiked too fast and said that if we complained, he'd leave us.

But then we got horribly lost. Darren, a boy my age, yelled to John that we were walking in circles. This made John mad, and he ordered Darren to go back to camp. The other boys argued about which way that was. More screaming. Three boys stomped away to try another trail. I rubbed away my tears and trudged behind Jeff.

After another hour, we were even more lost. We were in a tangle of thick trees, scraped by the brambles and poking tree limbs. John became strangely quiet, and the rest of us started to panic.

"HEELLLLPPP!" we screamed into the dense woods. I can still hear our yells echoing through the oaks. We were terrified. I thought we would die.

I wanted our parents to be searching for us, but I thought they probably were not. They were stoic German Lutherans—never alarmists. They were playing bridge in the sunshine, drinking mid-day Budweisers, talking about the gas shortage, using lake water to scrub bacon grease from the breakfast skillet, making Kool-Aid for dinner, hanging wet towels on our jump rope clothesline, and reading Agatha Christie. They didn't give us a thought.

My adrenaline was gone and only exhaustion remained. I sat in the dirt and cried. The heat, thirst, and walking had eroded my determination. I gave up and peed all over myself.

I can see myself on that dirty trail. I needed a hug, food, water, dry clothes, Band-Aids, a shower. I needed everything that I had no way of getting. Completely hopeless.

I carry that exact moment of helplessness with me. Even now, the sensations of my wet shorts, blinding dehydration, a headache, and breathless fear, anger, and terror are a splinter in my psyche.

What about you? What moment of overwhelming helplessness have you survived? When have you lost all comfort and control and been left with only panic, misery, rejection, and weakness? From here, on the ground, you can see everything you don't have. You're lost in the proverbial hot woods, exhausted, crying, starving, thirsty, and ashamed.

This is when you fully understand how dependent you are on God.

Eventually, our parents did look for us. I remember hearing them call and then running to my mom and crying, my relief and adrenaline colliding into sobs. Even those tough older boys fell into hugs from their parents. Our moms led us back to base camp and gave us water and Goldfish crackers, bandaged up our blisters, and handed us clean, dry clothes.

By the time we roasted marshmallows around the fire that night, the terrifying afternoon was already a story that we would retell a hundred times over the following decades. From the safety of that circle of friends, everything about that trek seemed ridiculous. Whose idea was it to go? Why didn't we take any water? The boys argued about who got us off track, and our parents muttered, "Thank God you're safe."

I've never forgotten that feeling of total helplessness. I'm feeling it now—the realization of my own weakness, my relief when help arrived, the faith that God will always help.

As in all the psalms—but especially in Psalm 116—we admit we need the Savior. We need the hope He provides, His love, His presence. We cannot do this on our own. It's through Christ's sacrifice and resurrection that we find hope. Even in our deepest helplessness, we are never abandoned.

ABOUT PSALM 116

Psalm 116 overflows with emotion. From the very first line, "I love the LORD, because He has heard my voice and my pleas for mercy" (v. 1), we can feel the relief of being rescued. We know that feeling well, the overwhelming gratitude that makes us want to cry out, "I will call on Him as long as I live" (v. 2).

Helpless, Yet Held

The psalmist vividly describes his desperation: "The snares of death encompassed me; the pangs of Sheol laid hold on me; I suffered distress and anguish" (v. 3). That's what true helplessness feels like—trapped, scared, unsure if we'll make it through. But God doesn't leave us there. When the psalmist cries out, "O LORD, I pray, deliver my soul!" (v. 4), God responds. We can't save ourselves, but He steps in, bringing hope and comfort and rescue.

God's Compassionate Response

In our weakest moments, God isn't detached. "Gracious is the LORD, and righteous; our God is merciful" (v. 5). He meets us with grace and kindness, never asking us to handle things alone.

Rest in His Goodness

Finally, the crisis ends, and we find relief. We can breathe again, knowing God has taken care of us. The psalmist's words in verse 7 ring true: "Return, O my soul, to your rest; for the LORD has dealt bountifully with you." Our heavenly Father wants us to find peace in His faithful care.

Ancient Hymn of Our Savior

Psalm 116 was part of the Hallel Psalms (Psalms 113–118) sung during Passover. Imagine Jesus singing these words, just as generations had done before Him. Imagine Him lifting His voice even as He prepared to face the cross. Knowing that Jesus trusted God's help in His darkest hour gives this psalm incredible significance. Jesus lived out the truth that God is present in our suffering, and, through His sacrifice, we experience God's everlasting love.

God's Love Is Always Enough

Psalm 116 reminds us of God's faithfulness. His grace meets us in our weakness, His mercy carries us through our struggles, and His love remains constant. This is not based on who we are but on who He is. Even when you feel helpless, remember this: God hears you, knows your heart, and stays with you. His love will always be enough.

DISCUSS PSALM 116

1. Share a moment when you felt helpless. How did your body react to the lack of control? Reflect on those feelings and what you experienced.

2. Reread Psalm 116. Which images or phrases resonate with your own experiences of helplessness?

PRAY

Heavenly Father, life often reveals our weaknesses. Please give me faith to trust You. Thank You for hearing my cries and lifting me up with Your love. Help me to see the ways You continually rescue me. In Jesus' name. Amen.

2. ANXIOUS

You Made Your Bed

For Mark, who quietly takes care of those he loves.

Psalm 23

1 The LORD is my shepherd; I shall not want.
2 He makes me lie down in green pastures.
He leads me beside still waters.
3 He restores my soul.
He leads me in paths of righteousness
for His name's sake.

4 Even though I walk through the valley of the shadow of death,
I will fear no evil,
for You are with me;
Your rod and Your staff,
they comfort me.

5 You prepare a table before me
in the presence of my enemies;
You anoint my head with oil;
my cup overflows.
6 Surely goodness and mercy shall follow me
all the days of my life,
and I shall dwell in the house of the LORD
forever.

At age 48, I found myself in a midlife crisis. I felt empty. Our oldest daughter had left for college. Our kids, who had needed so much for so many years, were now teenagers. I realized that one day they would all just *leave*. My husband, Mike, and I would be all alone.

Who would we become without the engine of our kids' needs propelling us?

Mike and I were both wrestling with that question one Saturday in October while we cleaned our vacation rental, Best of Times Beach House. For thirteen years, we had hosted thousands of guests at our Airbnb on Galveston Island, my hometown.

As I hosed sand off surf boards, those questions about my identity bobbed in my mind. I looked up to see a Realtor sticking a for-sale sign in front of the tall, skinny house across the street. We knew that house. Ten years earlier, we had watched the construction crew build it directly in front of ours.

"Hey!" Mike called to me from the upper deck. "Want to buy another beach house?"

"Ha. Right. Like we're playing Monopoly and buying up all the houses on the street," I yelled back.

Our family was in the most expensive season of our lives—one kid in college and three others headed there soon. We agonized over replacing the brakes on our old minivan. We didn't have hundreds of thousands of dollars for another beach house.

Except we were both struggling with something deeper than financial pressure. We were antsy for a purpose. And now Mike's idea was out there, right between us. We longed for direction that would push us to the next chapter. This could be it. We already knew how to run one vacation rental. Why not two?

So, we asked our Realtor to show us the tall house. Just for fun, just to daydream, just to snap us out of our current confusion. Inside, the beach house was stuffy and cluttered. We peeked in closets and measured bedrooms and murmured to each other the problems of turning this house into a short-term rental. It would take too much time and money. Impossible.

Or, maybe not? We desperately needed something to do. Maybe this house was a plot point that led to our next chapter?

Then, an HGTV-like montage of exciting real-estate moments occurred. We made a ridiculously low offer—so low that our Realtor warned us it would insult the sellers. Except, plot twist, they accepted it. Before we knew if we could pull this off, we were signing papers for a huge mortgage.

Then came *anxiety*.

You know this feeling: the constant drip of uncertainty pooling deep in you, creating puddles of fear, of anticipation, of regret, of buzzy, frantic worry. Growing out of those pools—like weeds, like pond ferns—was body-racking fear.

We carried this feeling in our guts as we signed papers on this illogical idea. We did not know how this could work. Fear made my jaw clench, my hands fidget, my eyes wild. I saw the same thing in Mike's face. Was this angst our new normal?

We stopped sleeping and worked instead. We quickly realized we hadn't found a mere plot twist; we'd found a tragedy. Unless we could figure out how to stop spending money and rent these houses out, we would have to sell one.

This new chapter in our lives made money weird. We owned two beach houses—and also scolded our kids when they ordered soda at Chick-fil-A instead of water. I felt so ashamed. The soundtrack playing in our heads was, *Do not fail, you irresponsible idiots. Work. Work. Work.*

And, oh, the problems with the new house. It had a weird, formal, outdated vibe. Dark wood floors, lace curtains, neglected areas. Everything was hard. Repairing broken deck boards and leaky faucets cost money we didn't have. We shopped thrift stores and clearance aisles for beachy decor and paid for it with credit cards we couldn't afford.

Every conversation between Mike and me was now "Hey. Did you finish the . . ." and every time, the answer was "No. I don't know how to do that." Fear enveloped us, and we snapped at each other. We numbed it by not looking directly at the real possibility this would end in a dumpster fire.

But some good news happened: friends showed up to help, families rented the house, we converted the attic into more living space, and the ocean view from the top floor was breathtaking. Great. Except I had become so used to the anxiety that the good news jarred me. I didn't trust it.

And here's the thing—when I shared my nightmare of gut-clenching anxiety with my friends, they weren't surprised. Everyone nodded and said, "Same." Constantly holding your breath? Of course. No sleep? Yep. Unable to eat but also bingeing a bag of Hershey's Kisses? Totally. Your neck muscles in knots? Just modern life.

This anxiety is our lives. The world is collectively holding its breath, clenching its jaw, fisting its hands, inhaling information, and picking its bleeding cuticles.

Oh, you too? What's causing you to clench your shoulders?

Your daughter needs therapy. You're drinking too much. Something is very wrong with a relationship, and you can't stop thinking about it. You never did all those things you said you would. You don't want to call the doctor about those weird symptoms. Your dad shouldn't live alone but can't move in with you.

You spent money you didn't have on a beach house.

What is this steady state of fear? Why are we all so terrified all the time? How can our bodies carry so much gut-twisting stress? Why have we all signed up for worry 24/7?

Throughout these anxiety-racked months, I turned to Psalm 23. These old, worn-out words comforted me—and they can comfort you. David's image of God as the perfect caretaker made me feel less alone. If everything falls apart, the Lord will still be *right here*. This is the peace we need under the weight of our snowballing nervousness.

Through this, I started to see my life and my problems differently. I stopped spending money we didn't have. One day, I turned off the "Add to Cart" part of my brain like an addict deletes his dealer's number. The torture of that anxiety changed me. Or, rather, God changed me through it.

I learned some very important lessons throughout this chapter of extreme anxiety. As the new beach house filled up with renters, as I learned how to manage money differently to pay for the mortgage, and as God continued to show me how to trust Him, I learned and relearned the truth I needed the whole time: I'm never alone.

Close your eyes and imagine the problems that are causing you anxiety right now. Feel the palpable worry in your body. Now, clench and release your fists. Breathe in and out. Sit for a few minutes, letting the details of this wash over you. Continue to breathe slowly.

Now, read David's words in Psalm 23 again. This time, know that God is leading you, His sheep. He is with you as you walk through the hard times. He takes perfect care of you. He will never, ever leave you.

ABOUT PSALM 23

Anxiety feels like a heavy weight pressing on your chest with endless what ifs running through your mind. But Psalm 23 offers a lifeline: the reminder that life is a journey, and God is your Shepherd. He's there to care for you, guide you, calm your fears, and lead you to a safe place.

Green Pastures & Still Waters

When we're anxious, we often try to control everything. But Psalm 23 invites us to release that need for control and trust God instead. "He makes me lie down in green pastures. He leads me beside still waters. He restores my soul" (vv. 2–3). Picture this: God leading you to a place of rest, knowing exactly what you need to feel at peace. You don't have to carry the weight of your worries alone.

Evil & Comfort

Psalm 23:4 holds special meaning for my son Nate. He chose it as his confirmation verse after a really tough eighth-grade year marked by the loss of a close friend. "Even though I walk through the valley of the shadow of death, I will fear no evil, for You are with me; Your rod and Your staff, they comfort me." This beloved verse captures both the deep pain we experience in this life and the comforting truth that God guides us, even in our darkest moments. It promises us that although we all will experience death, our Good Shepherd—Jesus—leads us to a place of calm, peaceful perfection with Him.

We will walk through pain and loss, but Jesus walks between us and evil. His sacrifice brings us salvation. Our thanksgiving isn't just a response to earthly blessings but to the eternal gift of grace.

Goodness & Mercy

This psalm wraps up with words that are a balm to anxious hearts: "Surely goodness and mercy shall follow me all the days of my life, and I shall dwell in the house of the LORD forever" (v. 6). Even when you're overwhelmed with fear or worry, God's love surrounds you. His goodness is a promise that follows you through every struggle, it will keep pursuing you every day of your life, and it promises you an eternal home with Him.

DISCUSS PSALM 23

1. How does knowing that God is your Shepherd bring comfort to your current worries or challenges?

2. What has Psalm 23 meant to you personally in difficult times?

PRAY

Lord, Shepherd, Father, thank You for being my constant source of care. Send Your Holy Spirit to comfort me when anxiety takes over. Give me strength and courage to face my fears, knowing You are always by my side. Strengthen my faith that You promise me a way through the darkness to safety and peace with You forever. In Jesus' name. Amen.

3. AWED

The Giraffe Behind the Curtain

For Marcilee, who loves family time at the cabin.

Psalm 65

1 Praise is due to You, O God, in Zion,
and to You shall vows be performed.
2 O You who hear prayer,
to You shall all flesh come.
3 When iniquities prevail against me,
You atone for our transgressions.
4 Blessed is the one You choose and bring near,
to dwell in Your courts!
We shall be satisfied with the goodness of Your house,
the holiness of Your temple!

5 By awesome deeds You answer us with righteousness,
O God of our salvation,
the hope of all the ends of the earth
and of the farthest seas;
6 the one who by His strength established the mountains,
being girded with might;
7 who stills the roaring of the seas,
the roaring of their waves,
the tumult of the peoples,
8 so that those who dwell at the ends of the earth are in awe at
Your signs.

You make the going out of the morning and the evening to shout for joy.

[9]You visit the earth and water it;
You greatly enrich it;
the river of God is full of water;
You provide their grain,
for so You have prepared it.
[10]You water its furrows abundantly,
settling its ridges,
softening it with showers,
and blessing its growth.
[11]You crown the year with Your bounty;
Your wagon tracks overflow with abundance.
[12]The pastures of the wilderness overflow,
the hills gird themselves with joy,
[13]the meadows clothe themselves with flocks,
the valleys deck themselves with grain,
they shout and sing together for joy.

We're smack dab in the middle of an "awe" story that's twenty years in the making. Well, I guess it's actually forty years in the making.

My husband grew up spending weekends at his family's lake house in Nebraska. He canoed across the lake as a kid, water-skied across it as a teenager, and hosted bonfires for his fraternity brothers as a college student. He loves the little stretch of sand in front of a glassy lake, next to the Platte River.

When we met after college, I fell in love with it too. It's a proper lake cabin—small and rustic and surrounded by pine trees. The fish are lazy and overfed but always willing to let you catch them and pose for a picture.

"The Cabin," as it's called in the Hergenrader family, fit well into whatever stage of life we were in. In our newlywed phase, it was the perfect place to invite our friends for a day of boating. But then, when we had kids, we learned the real beauty of the cabin: family vacations.

We piled our babies, bottles, diapers, two dogs, and everything else we could fit into our minivan and traveled sixteen hours to The Cabin. Mike and I stared numbly at the nine hundred miles of road while the kids stared at DVDs in the back seat.

The road never changed, and neither did The Cabin. The same friends and relatives visited, bringing the same Runza's and Valentino's pizza. The kids learned to swim, built sandcastles with their cousins, and caught toads, probably the same ones, every summer. We circled the lake in the pontoon boat and had the same conversations about who had a new dock or gazebo.

While this was the ideal vacation for kids too young to remember much, as our kids grew older, Mike and I began to worry. When Catie, our oldest, finished elementary school, we fretted that we had only six more summers together. If we wanted to snorkel amid coral, taste Maine lobster, hike the Grand Canyon, or a see a play on Broadway, we needed to get on it. Friends invited us to hike mountains in Breckenridge, to escape the Texas heat for a week in Canada, to finally take that epic Disney trip. It felt irresponsible to say no to all that just so we could ride in circles around the same lake.

Our kids were growing up and surprising us. Nate, our youngest, loved airplanes, and even at age 3, he navigated airports like a teenager. Sam talked constantly about an RV road trip. Elisabeth announced she wanted to be a missionary and wanted our family to do a service trip. And Catie wanted to travel with other people. We had outgrown The Cabin.

All this sounds ridiculous of course. Because, what? Who worries their kids are having too much family-centered lake fun? But we're all weak to the pressure to parent right. So, when the mom next door, whom you respect, is flying around the country with her daughter for dance competitions, and your work friend has taken up backpacking in the mountains with his son, it feels like you're being lazy by taking the same road trip.

But let me tell you the end of the story, or at least the delicious middle of it. For the next five years, we did go on all those big trips. We drove an RV across the desert, saw Times Square at night, gaped at the bald eagles off the coast of Canada, and watched the sun set over the Grand Canyon.

We also kept going to The Cabin. Every summer, we spent a few days of our vacation on that same stretch of sand, making the same circles in that boat, catching the same fish (or maybe their grandchildren), and water-skiing in the same arc that Mike had done for three decades.

Then, it was time for Catie to make a college decision. She looked at universities in California, Phoenix, and Texas. We were rooting for the school that would fit her best. I was betting on one in California—or the one close to home in Texas.

She surprised us all and announced she was going to school in Nebraska.

Nine hundred miles away from us.

But only one hour away from The Cabin.

I didn't see that coming. Yes, her grandparents would be close by. Yes, she wanted to become a teacher and the university she chose had an incredible program. But Nebraska? What about wanting to live by the mountains? What about wanting a big city experience?

Catie wanted to go to a place that felt like home. She wanted to ride around that same old lake in slow circles and have bonfires with her friends and watch sunsets over the Platte River. She wanted delicious familiarity.

Oh, I see it now. God was always preparing this place and this season for Catie. She left home at age 17 and grew up overnight. When she needed to burrow into her comfort zone, she drove herself to that same stretch of sand to rest.

This is what awe feels like. You expect to see the rabbit pop out of the hat and, instead, you get a giraffe coming from behind the curtain. Ah, *this*. You were doing it the whole time, Lord.

Psalm 68 describes this big-picture awe so beautifully. God nurtures everything. His abundance is everywhere. All of life is one large-scale moment of joy and wonder and completeness. Pay attention! Take a second to see what God is doing. You thought you were growing weeds—and God was growing sweet, huge watermelons.

We never actually know when we're at the start of a story or at the end. And that time was both for Catie. After three semesters, she left Nebraska and transferred to a school in Texas. She wanted to live in a bigger city, to be closer to family and her boyfriend, to be near her twin siblings who were starting high school, and to not face another Nebraska winter.

But the awe story stayed intact. Catie wanted to spend a year and a half near The Cabin because it's her favorite place. Then, as she matured, she realized that refuge would always be there for her. The best stories are the ones where we can see the awe unfold and keep unfolding. And that's what this story is for her. My response is to watch, wonder, and give thanks to the Lord, whose love lasts forever.

This is exactly the love we have in our Savior. All of human history centers around God's gift of His Son to us. As we witness the unfolding of this epic, divine narrative, we gasp at the unbelievable grace and ever-flowing love.

Look for awe in your life. It's right there in front of you: the exhilarating surprise, the deep breath of relief, the crackle of delight. Look at this harvest of what God is growing in your life. This is the delight that comes when you see His work in the world. Let it fill you with awe for His love that lasts and lasts and lasts.

ABOUT PSALM 65

Psalm 65 invites you to pause and be amazed by everything God is doing. It encourages you to step back and realize how small you are, in the best way possible. It's a reminder that Someone so much greater—so much more powerful—is holding everything together.

David wrote this psalm as a celebration, especially after a harvest, when God's faithfulness was obvious.

But Psalm 65 goes beyond harvests and nature. It's about seeing God's hand in every part of life. The grass that grows? That's God. The prayerful choice your daughter makes about her future? God's there too. Every piece of life is touched by His care.

God's Awe-some Deeds

David starts, "Praise is due to You, O God, in Zion, and to You shall vows be performed" (v. 1). Our response to God's faithfulness is simple but powerful: praise and trust. When we're weighed down by our mistakes, David reminds us that God's mercy is bigger: "When iniquities prevail against me, You atone for our transgressions" (v. 3). God's forgiveness is all about His loving character. Isn't that a reason to celebrate?

And then there's verse 5, where David describes God's power and love: "By awesome deeds You answer us with righteousness, O God of our salvation." This verse points specifically to Jesus, whose ultimate act of love on the cross is the greatest "awesome deed" of all.

Creator & Sustainer

Psalm 65 paints God as the magnificent Creator: "You visit the earth and water it; You greatly enrich it; the river of God is full of water" (v. 9).

Think about this: Jesus, the one through whom all things were made, walked on this very earth. He came to be with us, to show us His love in the most personal way. And He died to give us eternal life, taking care of us forever.

Perfect Care for You

Psalm 65 isn't just about mountains and rivers—it's about how God cares for you. He sustains the earth; He sustains your heart. He fills your life with good things because He loves you. Just as He sends rain to nourish the fields, He pours His love into your life, renewing you every day. And even more—He sends you His Son.

When you read Psalm 65, take a moment to really feel the awe. Be amazed, not just by the beauty around you but by how intricately God is involved in your life. He's a God of abundance, grace, constant care, and salvation. And the most incredible part? His awe-inspiring love never ends.

DISCUSS PSALM 65

1. What steals your sense of awe? Is it cynicism, doubt, or fatigue? Where do these "weeds" choke out your wonder? How could you live more open to God's work in your life?

2. Psalm 65:8–13 describes God's abundant care. Which image speaks to your heart the most? Why?

PRAY

Lord God, thank You for filling me with awe. Your care for the earth, Your people, and even the smallest details is amazing. Forgive me when I forget that my blessings come from You. Open my eyes to celebrate Your goodness. Keep delighting me with Your harvest in my life. In Jesus' name. Amen.

4. BROKENHEARTED

Is This the End?

For Theresa, who stands with the brokenhearted and for the hurting.

Psalm 34

1 I will bless the LORD at all times;
His praise shall continually be in my mouth.
2 My soul makes its boast in the LORD;
let the humble hear and be glad.
3 Oh, magnify the LORD with me,
and let us exalt His name together!

4 I sought the LORD, and He answered me
and delivered me from all my fears.
5 Those who look to Him are radiant,
and their faces shall never be ashamed.
6 This poor man cried, and the LORD heard him
and saved him out of all his troubles.
7 The angel of the LORD encamps
around those who fear Him, and delivers them.

8 Oh, taste and see that the LORD is good!
Blessed is the man who takes refuge in Him!
9 Oh, fear the LORD, you His saints,
for those who fear Him have no lack!
10 The young lions suffer want and hunger;
but those who seek the LORD lack no good thing.

[11]Come, O children, listen to me;
    I will teach you the fear of the LORD.
[12]What man is there who desires life
    and loves many days, that he may see good?
[13]Keep your tongue from evil
    and your lips from speaking deceit.
[14]Turn away from evil and do good;
    seek peace and pursue it.

[15]The eyes of the LORD are toward the righteous
    and His ears toward their cry.
[16]The face of the LORD is against those who do evil,
    to cut off the memory of them from the earth.
[17]When the righteous cry for help, the LORD hears
    and delivers them out of all their troubles.
[18]The LORD is near to the brokenhearted
    and saves the crushed in spirit.

[19]Many are the afflictions of the righteous,
    but the LORD delivers him out of them all.
[20]He keeps all his bones;
    not one of them is broken.
[21]Affliction will slay the wicked,
    and those who hate the righteous will be condemned.
[22]The LORD redeems the life of His servants;
    none of those who take refuge in Him will be condemned.

We all remember our worst breakup. Mine was with my college boyfriend, the one I'd pictured a whole future with. Looking back now, I can't recall many details about the relationship itself—our routines, our inside jokes—but I remember exactly how it felt to have my heart broken.

It was disorienting, like suddenly being untethered from everything I thought was certain. The dreams we had woven together felt less like unfulfilled plans and more like pieces of myself slipping away. If you've been through that kind of heartbreak, you know it leaves you questioning who you are, feeling hollow, and wondering if you'll feel whole again.

But in college, there was another breakup I witnessed that taught me a lesson I'll never forget.

My friend Hannah was vibrant, magnetic, and confident in that effortless way that made you think she'd been a cheerleader in high school. She was fun and loved Jesus, but she didn't take anything too seriously. During our freshman year, she dated a few guys, each of whom fell hard for her. None of them kept her attention though.

Then she met one of the most admired guys on our small, Christian college campus. He was the whole package: athletic, deeply spiritual, and charismatic in a way that made everyone take notice. Everyone who knew him admired his strength and his unwavering faith. Hannah was no exception. She fell for him hard.

Their relationship transfixed and transformed her. Suddenly, she was walking to church on Sundays, something she hadn't done before. They met nightly in the dorm common room to read Galatians together, dreaming of a future where their hearts would burn for the Lord even more than for each other. From the start, they talked about getting married and having a family. This looked like lifelong love.

Then came the fight. It started with his small, condescending comment. Something petty. She yelled and accused him of being controlling. He walked away and gave her the silent treatment for days. She made a public scene, and he told her they were finished.

The breakup left Hannah shattered. She locked herself in her dorm room, ignoring our knocks and pleas to let us in. The girl who had once been so full of light now seemed swallowed up by darkness.

Three days later, she finally opened the door. We expected a disaster—a room mirroring the chaos we knew she felt inside. Instead, it was spotless. Except for the notes. All over her room were hundreds of pieces of paper, index cards, and sticky notes. They were plastered across the walls, on the floor, and even on her pillow. Each one had the same verse: "The LORD is near to the brokenhearted and saves the crushed in spirit" (Psalm 34:18).

Hannah had written and rewritten that verse, from different translations, trying to carve it into her heart. The Message version read, "If your heart is broken, you'll find GOD right there; if you're kicked in the gut, he'll help you catch your breath." The Good News Translation said, "The LORD is near to those who are discouraged; he saves those who have lost all hope" (GNT). Her room was transformed into a sanctuary of hope, where she was clinging to the only truth she had.

Seeing those words scattered around her room hit me. The Bible verse was a physical reminder that, in our deepest pain, when we feel rejected, confused, or terrified about the future, God is near. When your spirit feels crushed under the weight of grief or rejection, He's right there, closer than you can imagine.

Heartbreak comes in so many forms. It is not just romantic relationships; it is the devastating phone call from the doctor, a friendship that ends, the death of someone you loved, or the realization that your dream job isn't yours after all. The emotions are universal: shock, betrayal, sadness, fear, hopelessness. Your spirit feels heavy, almost broken.

But Psalm 34:18 promises something incredible: God is close to the brokenhearted. Hannah clung to that truth back in 1992, and I've clung to it a million times since. God's nearness in those moments and in those words is profoundly comforting.

Hannah never reconciled with that guy, but the experience changed her. She emerged from it with a deeper understanding of God's faithfulness in the darkest moments.

In my own heartbreaks, I remember Hannah's room and all those verses. I remember that God has compassion for every tear, hears every broken prayer, and stays close. Heartbreak comes in all shapes and forms, but His presence never wavers.

David understood this when he wrote Psalm 34. He wanted us to know that God is always still God, even when our world shatters. God is as close as a whispered prayer, as steady as His promise that He will never leave. Even in the darkness, even when you feel broken beyond repair, God is near, and that truth can be the light that guides you through.

ABOUT PSALM 34

Heartbreak is one of the hardest journeys to navigate. You try to piece things together, but it only makes your weaknesses more apparent. This is when you realize just how much you need God.

Psalm 34 meets you right there, in that brokenness. This psalm is a gift for desperate times, a reminder that when life leaves you feeling like you've hit the bottom, God's presence is your hope.

Always Good

David wrote Psalm 34 in the middle of his own nightmare. He was running for his life from King Abimelech, forced to pretend he was insane just to survive. He didn't know if he'd make it through. Desperate, he turned to God.

Praise Him Continually

Despite his fear, David starts with praise: "I will bless the LORD at all times; His praise shall continually be in my mouth" (v. 1). Can you imagine? Worshiping God when you're in that place? When it feels impossible to even lift your head, let alone sing praises. But David's words are a reminder that God is the shelter for our souls.

We're the Brokenhearted

One of the most comforting verses in the Bible is Psalm 34:18: "The LORD is near to the brokenhearted and saves the crushed in spirit." David knew this truth deeply. He knew that God promises He will not turn away from our weakness. God is not disappointed when we're struggling. He is the balm for our heart.

Let yourself feel the pain of heartbreak. Don't rush past the grief or numb yourself to the sadness. It's okay to sit with those emotions and feel them all. Because in that raw vulnerability, when you know you are weak and broken, you can also know God's power to heal.

I Cried. God Heard.

David writes, "This poor man cried, and the LORD heard him and saved him out of all his troubles" (v. 6). David doesn't rely on himself or his strength. He surrenders: "I cried." And God heard. Know that you don't have to do this alone. God listens and responds with exactly what you need.

Weary, Burdened, Brokenhearted

Jesus echoes this in Matthew 11:28: "Come to Me, all who labor and are heavy laden, and I will give you rest." He invites us to bring our broken hearts to Him. He knows our pain and offers to carry it for us. We can lean into Him for comfort.

The Promise

Psalm 34 continues with a promise: "When the righteous cry for help, the LORD hears and delivers them out of all their troubles" (v. 17). God is here, right now. He is our refuge, our healer, our hope. Come to Him, exactly as you are—worn out, brokenhearted, exhausted—and let Him carry you.

DISCUSS PSALM 34

1. What does it mean to you that God is "near to the brokenhearted" (v. 18)?

2. Share about a time when you felt crushed in spirit and experienced God's presence and comfort.

PRAY

Lord, thank You for being so near when my heart is broken. You see my pain and bring Your healing. Help me trust Your everlasting love, even when I'm hurting. Give me the courage to rely on Your care and the strength to face my struggles with You by my side. In Jesus' name. Amen.

Wisdom Psalms

So teach us to number our days that we may get a heart of wisdom. Psalm 90:12

Wisdom Psalms teach us to look for God's truth in the middle of life's confusion and the world's lies. This type of wisdom is different from the information we inhale in our modern culture. This is about finding direction rooted in God's character.

Wisdom is God's Law that shows us His perfect nature. Wisdom gives you a steady place to stand when the world around you shifts. Wisdom, rooted in God's love and truth, directs your steps, becoming the light that leads you. May these psalms show you how His wisdom shapes each season, every emotion, and all experiences with purpose.

Waiting with Hope (Psalm 40)

Read Psalm 40 in your seasons of longing. David shares the wisdom of waiting, encouraging you to wait "patiently for the LORD" (v. 1). It feels like nothing is happening, but God is tilling the soil of your life. He is preparing you for growth you cannot see or imagine.

Planted by Streams (Psalm 1)

In this first psalm, God tells us wisdom is living in the Law of the Lord. You're invited to see yourself "like a tree planted by streams of water" (v. 3). You flourish when you're rooted in the nutrients of God's love and His Word. You feel different from those around you. Grounded in God, you stand strong regardless of the changing seasons.

The Power of Wisdom (Psalm 139)

Psalm 139 brings God's wisdom from the universal to the individual.

In these words, wisdom becomes deeply personal as we learn that we are known, valued, and worthy. Verse 14 tells us, "I praise You, for I am fearfully and wonderfully made." In a world that questions your worth, this psalm assures you of God's intentional design in every part of your life.

The Gift of Connection (Psalm 133)

Psalm 133 shifts the focus from your individual journey to the beauty of being connected with others. We live in an era of isolation. Friendships get canceled, we spend too much time online, and we feel disconnected. But this psalm paints a powerful picture: "how good and pleasant it is" when God's people come together (v. 1). This ancient bond is sacred. Psalm 133 invites you to imagine what divine unity feels like.

Together in Wisdom

These psalms show you how God's truth can guide your life. Psalm 40 teaches patience when you feel left behind. Psalm 1 encourages us to embrace our uniqueness as God's people. Psalm 139 reminds us of our worth in His love. And Psalm 133 celebrates unity with the Lord.

Write Your Own Wisdom Psalm

This is the place to share the lessons life has taught you. Write down the raw truths about what you've witnessed. Put words to the things God has shown you about living well, trusting Him, and finding hope. Let your images, your experiences, and your words capture the guidance He gives you in His Word.

1. Bring your whole heart.

What is weighing you down right now? Are you feeling sad, scared, or stuck? Start by bringing those real thoughts and feelings to God. Wisdom Psalms come from honest hearts. Picture yourself talking to a friend who gets you. God is right here, listening.

2. Paint a picture of God's wisdom.

What does God's wisdom feel like? Maybe it's light cutting through fog or rain settling the dust. Use images that show how you need Jesus. Let your words flow. The power is in processing your experiences to understand who He is.

3. Get real about hard stuff.

What struggles have been the hardest for you? What questions do you have for God? What have you not understood about Him or His plan for you? Lay all these out. Don't hide from the messiness of life. Let yourself see God in it.

4. Hold tight to who God is.

Write about the parts of God's character that ground you. What stories in the Bible resonate most with you? Is it where you see His kindness, His love, His strength? Wisdom Psalms anchor us to our God's everlasting love. These truths bring peace to your heart. They remind you that God's wisdom is steady when the summit feels far away and the valleys feel overwhelming. His love anchors you through every climb and every descent, teaching you to trust His path.

5. End with a flicker of hope.

Close your psalm with trust, even if it's just a spark. Picture God holding you through every unknown. Wisdom Psalms remind us that God's got this. Let your words, your praise, your requests rest in your Savior. He hears you and is with you.

5. IMPATIENT

Wait. What?

For Michelle, who prayed for me to find inspiration.

Psalm 40

1 I waited patiently for the LORD;
He inclined to me and heard my cry.
2 He drew me up from the pit of destruction,
out of the miry bog,
and set my feet upon a rock,
making my steps secure.
3 He put a new song in my mouth,
a song of praise to our God.
Many will see and fear,
and put their trust in the LORD.

4 Blessed is the man who makes
the LORD his trust,
who does not turn to the proud,
to those who go astray after a lie!
5 You have multiplied, O LORD my God,
Your wondrous deeds and Your thoughts toward us;
none can compare with You!
I will proclaim and tell of them,
yet they are more than can be told.

6 In sacrifice and offering You have not delighted,
but You have given me an open ear.

Burnt offering and sin offering
You have not required.
7Then I said, "Behold, I have come;
in the scroll of the book it is written of me:
8I delight to do Your will, O my God;
Your law is within my heart."

9I have told the glad news of deliverance
in the great congregation;
behold, I have not restrained my lips,
as You know, O LORD.
10I have not hidden Your deliverance within my heart;
I have spoken of Your faithfulness and Your salvation;
I have not concealed Your steadfast love and Your faithfulness
from the great congregation.

11As for You, O LORD, You will not restrain
Your mercy from me;
Your steadfast love and Your faithfulness will
ever preserve me!
12For evils have encompassed me
beyond number;
my iniquities have overtaken me,
and I cannot see;
they are more than the hairs of my head;
my heart fails me.

13Be pleased, O LORD, to deliver me!
O LORD, make haste to help me!
14Let those be put to shame and disappointed altogether
who seek to snatch away my life;
let those be turned back and brought to dishonor
who delight in my hurt!
15Let those be appalled because of their shame
who say to me, "Aha, Aha!"

16But may all who seek You
rejoice and be glad in You;

> may those who love Your salvation
> say continually, "Great is the LORD!"
> 17 As for me, I am poor and needy,
> but the LORD takes thought for me.
> You are my help and my deliverer;
> do not delay, O my God!

For the past three years, writing has felt like a blank space. After producing books, articles, and devotions like clockwork for twenty-five years, the words just stopped. It was as if I had been plunged into a wilderness—dark, isolated, and empty. Every day at 4:00 a.m., I'd sit at my computer and ask God to bring back the inspiration. But the screen stayed blank. His silence was deafening.

The hardest part? Feeling powerless. Watching other writers come up with brilliant metaphors and life-giving devotionals while I was stuck. I was like the barren fig tree from Jesus' parable in Luke 13, taking up space but producing no fruit. In the story that Jesus tells, a landowner wanted to cut down a fig tree that hadn't borne fruit for years. But the gardener pleaded for more time: "Sir, let it alone this year also, until I dig around it and put on manure. Then if it should bear fruit next year, well and good; but if not, you can cut it down" (Luke 13:8–9). I resonated with that fig tree, sure I was no longer useful, so frustrated I couldn't seem to bear fruit.

Maybe you know that feeling too—that strange mix of stress and helplessness, of wanting so desperately to move forward but being completely stuck. Waiting, like David describes in Psalm 40, can feel embarrassing and excruciating. It's as though everyone else is sprinting ahead while you stand frozen. The uncertainty is what makes it so hard, the not knowing when or if things will change.

In my long season of waiting, I still showed up, even when it felt excruciating. I wrote early drafts of this book. I wrote a novel that no one will probably ever read. I coached other writers with their projects. I met with teenagers who were struggling with their faith.

I spoke to groups, taught classes, and asked everyone to pray for the words to come again. And I waited.

Eventually, God began to give me words again, and then this book started to take real shape. He answered my prayers through encouraging friends and unexpected help. He was teaching me a lesson I never wanted to learn: total dependence on Him. Letting go of self-imposed expectations. Surrendering my timeline. Trusting that He would provide what I needed, when I needed it, how I needed it. Just like the gardener in Jesus' parable, God was patiently tending to me, working on my roots even when I couldn't see the growth.

This is the gift waiting offers. It strips away the illusion that we can control anything and teaches us to lean into God's perfect timing. Even when we feel like barren fig trees, God is working the soil. The delay isn't punishment; it is preparation.

Maybe you're waiting too. Waiting for healing, for a relationship to be restored, or to find your purpose. The waiting feels unbearable, but Psalm 40 reminds us of these truths: God hears your cries. He lifts you out of the pit and sets your feet on solid ground. The wait feels endless, but God is at work, even when you can't see it.

So, what do we do in the waiting? We worship. Write a psalm. Pray. Sing a hymn. Take a nap. Read the Bible. Trust that God is weaving something beautiful in the background, even when we don't understand. Let Him dig around the roots of your heart, tending to you in ways you can't yet comprehend.

During this experience, determine to trust God's provision. Delight in the ways He has cared for you in the past. Write down those stories. Remember that even in seasons of barrenness God is preparing new growth.

And just as the gardener in Jesus' parable asked for one more year to tend the fig tree, God is making long-term plans for your life. The waiting will end. The barren places will one day bear fruit. God will provide an answer or a way. And through it all, you will learn a beautiful lesson: Time is never wasted. That's because God is giving you the time. It's part of His grand plan for your life here and your life forever with Him.

ABOUT PSALM 40

In Psalm 40, David captures the agony of waiting. David also offers us a gentle but profound reminder: God's timing is always perfect, even if it feels painfully slow or unfair or lonely.

Step by Step

Interestingly, Psalm 40 shows the unfolding of God's plan in a way that mirrors the slow, sometimes excruciating steps of waiting. David's words are a journey, reflecting how faith develops over time. He describes being lifted from the "pit of destruction" and set upon a rock (v. 2), emphasizing that God's work is intentional, not rushed and not random.

Waiting on the Lord

Psalm 40 guides us to shift our focus from the narrow view of our impatience to the long view of God's faithfulness: "He put a new song in my mouth, a song of praise to our God" (v. 3). The waiting may feel unbearable, but David's story and the parable of the fig tree both remind us that God does act. His timing is worth every moment we spend waiting. The psalm helps us transform waiting from an agonizing pause into an active posture of hope and trust.

And Still, We Wait

Throughout Scripture, David speaks often of waiting patiently. In Psalm 27, he urges, "Wait for the LORD; be strong, and let your heart take courage" (v. 14). His words show a deep understanding of God's timeline, which rarely aligns with our own. In Psalm 40, David's testimony is personal; he experienced firsthand that God's timing is worth the wait.

DISCUSS PSALM 40

1. What are you impatient for right now? Write out what makes you feel anxious for it to happen.

2. What can you do while you are waiting for God to change your circumstances?

PRAY

Lord, be with me. Hear me crying out in frustration and fear. You are close, dear Lord. You are with me as I wait. You will never, ever leave me. Remind me of the comfort You have given to all those who have felt like this. Remind me of the hope that You give through my Savior, Jesus. Amen.

6. DIFFERENT

Robes, Wine & Supper

For my Elisabeth, who lives differently and is a missionary to all of us.

Psalm 1

1 Blessed is the man
    who walks not in the counsel of the wicked,
nor stands in the way of sinners,
    nor sits in the seat of scoffers;
2 but his delight is in the law of the LORD,
    and on His law he meditates day and night.

3 He is like a tree
    planted by streams of water
that yields its fruit in its season,
    and its leaf does not wither.
In all that he does, he prospers.
4 The wicked are not so,
    but are like chaff that the wind drives away.

5 Therefore the wicked will not stand in the judgment,
    nor sinners in the congregation of the righteous;
6 for the LORD knows the way of the righteous,
    but the way of the wicked will perish.

If you've ever been to an all-inclusive resort, you know the scene: endless buffets, cocktails brought right to your chair, indulgence around every corner. It's an escape designed to drown out daily stress, a world where nothing matters but how relaxed you feel in the sun. Sunburned tourists sip sugary drinks, hoping the excess can fill whatever emptiness they've brought with them.

To be clear, I've always loved these resorts. When Mike and I were newlyweds, we saved for vacations like that—dancing on the beaches of Jamaica, playing in the waves in Mexico, unwinding by the pool with piña coladas. When our kids got old enough to travel, we went on several trips like this with Mike's parents and his brother's family. And we all loved them.

But then we took a different kind of trip. I was invited to teach the Bible studies at a retreat for missionaries serving across Latin America. The retreat was held at an all-inclusive resort in the Dominican Republic—familiar yet so different from our past vacations. Instead of swimsuits, I packed church clothes. Instead of a beach read, I carried my Bible. Instead of flip-flops, I packed books for the missionaries. I thought I was there to encourage them, but God had something else to teach me.

From the moment we arrived, the contrast was striking. Dressed for worship, we made our way past sunbathing tourists while they lounged poolside. Our group moved through the resort, past the discarded cocktail glasses and burger baskets on our way to celebrate the Lord's Supper. I had been where they were, but this time was different.

I have always known what it means to live differently. When I was growing up, we skipped secular Sunday activities to be in church. We set aside time for rest, for God. My parents didn't value material things. We drove an old car, didn't wear trendy clothes, and lived simply. But I remember that, back then, I prayed for contentment with God's provision while envying those who seemed to have it all. In those moments of envy, life seemed easier for them. I've learned since then that trusting in God might not be easier but it's so much better.

Psalm 1 describes this perfectly: “He is like a tree planted by streams of water that yields its fruit in its season, and its leaf does not wither” (v. 3). God’s Word is that stream—life-giving, sustaining, grounding in a way that temporary pleasures never are. So many of us chase fleeting indulgences, things that slip through our fingers. God offers something lasting.

Chaff, as verse 4 describes, is the empty excess that blows away—the distractions, the shallow pleasures. These things look appealing, but chaff can never nourish and sustain us. God’s presence, His Word, is the living water that quenches our deepest thirst.

During the retreat, as the missionaries prayed and sang, I was struck by how deeply rooted they were in this truth. They weren’t seeking an escape because they had already found the source of true fulfillment. Despite their economic struggles, they were filled with the richness of God’s presence. They weren’t there for the peace of a good vacation. They had the peace of knowing they were planted by streams of living water.

That’s what we all need. Not another distraction or indulgence but the deep waters of God’s love. We’re all searching for something that lasts. The world offers us chaff—temporary thrills that disappear with the wind. But God offers real nourishment and peace. Once you’ve tasted that, you know the difference. You realize it’s the only thing that truly satisfies and truly lasts.

In the end, everything else fades. But God’s Word, His wisdom, His love? They last. They are what we were made for.

ABOUT PSALM 1

Psalm 1 opens with a proclamation: “Blessed is the man who walks not in the counsel of the wicked, nor stands in the way of sinners, nor sits in the seat of scoffers” (v. 1). It reminds us that as God’s people we’re different.

Streams of Water

Imagine a tree planted beside a steady stream, its roots drawing nourishment and strength from ever-flowing waters. The tree thrives, not because it tries hard but because it's connected to a reliable source of life. That's the kind of security God offers us—His love is the reliable source that sustains us through every season.

Chaff That the Wind Drives Away

Psalm 1 paints a vivid contrast: "The wicked are not so, but are like chaff that the wind drives away" (v. 4). Chaff—light, hollow, and blown around without purpose—reminds us how chasing shallow things leaves us. But the tree? It's solid, deeply rooted, and full of life.

Meditating on God's Word

This psalm invites us to live differently: "His delight is in the law of the LORD, and on His law he meditates day and night" (v. 2). This kind of meditation means soaking in God's Word, letting it settle deep into your heart and change you from the inside out.

Pointing Us to Christ

Psalm 1 also points us to Christ, who bears eternal fruit. "For the LORD knows the way of the righteous, but the way of the wicked will perish" (v. 6). Jesus—the Living Water—shows us the strength and peace that come from being rooted in Him.

Root Yourself in God's Love

Psalm 1 is a beautiful reminder that God's love never runs dry. It's like a steady, life-giving stream, nourishing us no matter what season we're in. We don't have to get swept away by fear or the world's empty pleasures because God's love is more than enough.

DISCUSS PSALM 1

1. How does Psalm 1 help you embrace feeling different because of your faith and values?

2. In what ways can you stay rooted in God's Word to find strength when you feel different from those around you?

PRAY

Lord, thank You for guiding me with Your Word and for the blessings You give me through it. When I feel different from those around me, help me to find strength and confidence in You. Remind me that being set apart for You is joy. Keep me rooted in Your love and truth. In Your Son's name. Amen.

7. WORTHY

Leftover Fish or a Seat at the Table

For Catie, trust your own worth is in Christ alone.

Psalm 139

1 O LORD, You have searched me and known me!
2 You know when I sit down and when I rise up;
    You discern my thoughts from afar.
3 You search out my path and my lying down
    and are acquainted with all my ways.
4 Even before a word is on my tongue,
    behold, O LORD, You know it altogether.
5 You hem me in, behind and before,
    and lay Your hand upon me.
6 Such knowledge is too wonderful for me;
    it is high; I cannot attain it.

7 Where shall I go from Your Spirit?
    Or where shall I flee from Your presence?
8 If I ascend to heaven, You are there!
    If I make my bed in Sheol, You are there!
9 If I take the wings of the morning
    and dwell in the uttermost parts of the sea,
10 even there Your hand shall lead me,
    and Your right hand shall hold me.
11 If I say, "Surely the darkness shall cover me,
    and the light about me be night,"

12 even the darkness is not dark to You;
the night is bright as the day,
for darkness is as light with You.

13 For You formed my inward parts;
You knitted me together in my mother's womb.
14 I praise You, for I am fearfully and wonderfully made.
Wonderful are Your works;
my soul knows it very well.
15 My frame was not hidden from You,
when I was being made in secret,
intricately woven in the depths of the earth.
16 Your eyes saw my unformed substance;
in Your book were written, every one of them,
the days that were formed for me,
when as yet there was none of them.

17 How precious to me are Your thoughts, O God!
How vast is the sum of them!
18 If I would count them, they are more than the sand.
I awake, and I am still with You.

19 Oh that You would slay the wicked, O God!
O men of blood, depart from me!
20 They speak against You with malicious intent;
Your enemies take Your name in vain.
21 Do I not hate those who hate You, O LORD?
And do I not loathe those who rise up against You?
22 I hate them with complete hatred;
I count them my enemies.

23 Search me, O God, and know my heart!
Try me and know my thoughts!
24 And see if there be any grievous way in me,
and lead me in the way everlasting!

A million years ago, I worked as a waitress in a seafood institution. A Galveston legend, Gaido's wasn't just a restaurant—

it was an experience. Tourists flocked there, drawn by white tablecloths, tuxedo-clad servers, and little bowls of warm water for rinsing stinky fingers after feasting. For more than one hundred years, the Gaido family had been perfecting seafood dinners for those willing to pay for the best.

Gaido's was massive, seating as many as 250 guests in a single night. The waitstaff life was cutthroat, fast-paced, and relentless. If a server hustled hard enough, he or she could pocket hundreds in tips. But it was brutal work. Balancing trays piled high with seafood platters that weighed more than your arms could handle. Smiling as you handled four or five tables at once, taking orders, answering questions, changing orders, and listening to complaints about the twelve-dollar dessert.

That summer job taught me so much. Mostly, it taught me how far I would go to belong.

The regular servers worked year-round and treated summer kids like outsiders. As a summer kid, I was just passing through, a temporary annoyance. To win their approval, I followed implicit rules. Arrive early to snag the best section. Refill everyone's water glasses, not just those at my tables. Help with their trays. And never, ever question them when they ate off their customers' plates.

I know. Revolting.

Let me paint a picture. Gaido's red snapper was a delicate, white fish lightly dusted with Parmesan, drizzled with rich butter, and sprinkled with zesty lemon. But the real indulgence was the fresh lump crab meat heaped on top. This melt-in-your-mouth creation—crispy, tender, grilled to perfection—wasn't just food. It was art. A bite of heaven, caught that morning, grilled to golden perfection, ready to dissolve on your tongue.

Most of the diners couldn't finish. The richness overwhelmed them. Plates came back half-eaten, and those who were tourists couldn't take the leftovers back to their hotel rooms. We cleared hundreds of plates of half-eaten food abandoned by newlyweds too busy gazing into each other's eyes, families wrangling toddlers, retirees about to embark on a cruise, sunburned teenagers who would rather be anywhere else.

That leftover food made its way to the servers' alley—a cramped metal counter where we could observe the dining room through a long window. The customers carried on, blissfully unaware we watched them like seagulls, waiting for their discarded food.

The veteran servers would slice away the parts touched by a fork and indulge in the snapper that was so fresh it had been swimming a few hours before.

At first, I was appalled. But the job wears you down. Eight-hour shifts leave you starving; the scent of butter and lemon filling the air calls to you. It's easy to justify. The food is too good to waste. You're too tired to care. Everyone's doing it.

So, there I was, in line with the others, eating seafood off strangers' plates. And you know what? I didn't even feel that bad. I wanted to fit in. I wanted to belong. And if that meant eating someone else's leftovers, so be it.

We all do it, don't we? Maybe not with food. But we consume the garbage around us. We watch TV shows that glorify what we know is wrong. We spread gossip to feel self-righteous. We scroll through endless social media reels, numbing our brains. We eat junk, drink too much caffeine and wine, and let our souls absorb the empty things the world throws at us.

And all of this changes us. It makes us feel unworthy.

Eating leftovers made me feel ashamed. It wasn't like sharing a piece of chocolate cake with friends. There was no joy. No celebration. We didn't talk about it. While we ate, we watched the diners through that window. We felt a world apart from them.

Then, one night, my boyfriend flew into town and we went to Gaido's for dinner. I wore a flowery dress I'd bought just for his visit. He wore khakis and a crisp, white shirt. My friend Maria, the hostess, seated us at a cozy, candlelit table with a view of the Gulf.

I ordered snapper. He ordered crab cakes. And as we settled into our romantic dinner, I knew the servers were watching us from the other side of the glass. They were eating someone else's discarded food while I was served fresh, beautiful seafood prepared just for me.

It hit me then. What we consume changes us. It shapes how we see ourselves. When we settle for garbage, we start to believe that's all we're worth.

Every time we stay silent when we should speak up, every time we let the cynicism win, and every time we hustle when we should rest, we send ourselves a message: *You don't deserve better than this.*

But you do.

What if you believed God when He said He designed you with love and care? What if you trusted that your value isn't determined by the chaos around you? What if you knew, deep in your soul, that you were created for more?

What if you treated yourself like you were worth the forty-dollar snapper?

Imagine carrying that love into every part of your day. Reading God's Word and feeding your spirit rather than doomscrolling. Praying instead of worrying. Thanking God rather than asking for more.

The psalmist tells us that God knew us before we were formed. Every detail of our being, He knows and cherishes. God cares about how we treat ourselves—not just our bodies but our hearts, our minds, our souls.

You are not a garbage disposal. You are fearfully and wonderfully made. God gives you His very best—Jesus.

This is the message of Psalm 139. It's a love letter written to you. Over and over, God says, *"You are worthy."*

ABOUT PSALM 139

Psalm 139 is God's beautiful reminder that He knows and loves you more than you can imagine. Do you believe that? Know that God created you with precise intention.

You Are Known

The psalm begins with this good news: "O LORD, You have searched me and known me!" (v. 1). He is an intimate God, who sees your thoughts, your hopes, and your struggles. And the best part? He still loves you completely.

Verse 13 paints such a beautiful picture: "For You formed my inward parts; You knitted me together in my mother's womb." I love the image of God knitting us together. Every stitch planned, counted, and intentional, He carefully and lovingly put every part of us in place. Even the parts of ourselves we might struggle to accept He crafted with purpose.

Both Powerful & Intimate

For thousands of years, Psalm 139 has brought comfort to people who need to be reminded of their value. Our God is powerful enough to run the whole world and loving enough to know each of us intimately.

Love Fully Revealed

In Christ, we see God's love fully revealed. Jesus came close, living among us, feeling our struggles, and walking alongside us. He suffered like we do. He prayed the same psalms we do. Our Savior showed us what real, human, up-close love looks like.

DISCUSS PSALM 139

1. When do you feel worthless? What do you do when you feel worthless that makes it worse? Why do you do this?

2. What does the phrase "fearfully and wonderfully made" mean to you?

PRAY

Heavenly Father, Creator of everything, thank You for knowing me so intimately and for making me with perfect care and precise purpose. When I feel unworthy, help me to remember that I am fearfully and wonderfully made by You. Fill my heart with the assurance of Your love and the knowledge of my value in Your eyes. In Jesus' name. Amen.

8. DISCONNECTED

I'm Fine & I Can't Breathe

For Melissa, my praying (and parenting) sister for many, many years.

Psalm 133

[1]Behold, how good and pleasant it is
    when brothers dwell in unity!
[2]It is like the precious oil on the head,
    running down on the beard,
on the beard of Aaron,
    running down on the collar of his robes!
[3]It is like the dew of Hermon,
    which falls on the mountains of Zion!
For there the LORD has commanded the blessing,
    life forevermore.

There's really only one way to handle the Texas heat in the middle of the summer: leave.

So, for the past few summers, when our kids were too old for VBS but too young for full-time jobs, we escaped to the mountains. Our tradition was to head to Breckenridge, Colorado, with our dear friends, the Brignacs, who also have two teenagers. Together, we'd do whatever we could to revel in the cooler air, a refreshing break from the suffocating southern heat back home, which feels like sitting inside a damp dryer.

In that brisk mountain climate, something changes in all of us. We're invigorated, suddenly game for ten-mile bike rides, zip line adventures, early morning fishing trips, and swims in the icy mountain streams. What keeps us coming back year after year, though, is the hiking. And every summer, our teens push for something longer, harder, more epic.

Our teenagers think they can handle these hikes on their own. They crave independence, rushing ahead and breaking free from the slow pace of their parents. But that independence is risky. They don't fully realize how quickly things can turn dangerous. Mountain storms make us huddle together for safety. Careless steps can result in injury. Leaving the trail makes you vulnerable to getting lost.

Just like in life, trying to go it alone can lead to trouble. As much as we want to prove ourselves, we know that hiking—and life—require the steady strength and support of community.

The mountains are not forgiving. This past summer, when our kids insisted on tackling a fourteener, we chose Quandary Peak. Fourteeners are mountains with an elevation of at least fourteen thousand feet above sea level. They demand more than just stamina; they test the hiker's resolve and body in every way. Climbing one of these peaks means dealing with the altitude, where even simple tasks can leave you breathless. Your muscles ache, your mind gets fuzzy, and every step feels heavier than the last. Coming down is equally grueling, with loose rocks and steep descents that punish tired legs.

Therefore, Quandary isn't a hike you tackle solo, especially for those who live at sea level like we do. The oxygen depletion at peak elevation can disorient you, make you delirious, and leave you feeling panicked. You need your people. You need to check in with one another, share water, keep the pace steady, and encourage one another when the challenge seems like it will break your spirit.

And so, we hike together, even our kids. We pause at every breathtaking vista, checking in with one another, marveling at the creation around us. The reward for our slow, deliberate pace is experiencing the beauty together, standing shoulder to shoulder, soaking in the 360-degree views of jagged rock formations, deep tree groves, and sunlit trails that look like a painting.

These moments make me think of Psalm 133 and the power of genuine connection. But staying connected isn't always easy. Like our teenagers who are eager to leave, life's demands and our own stubborn independence make us isolate ourselves. But we're not meant to. God created us to need one another. He created us for community so that when life gets hard—when the trail is steep, when the air is thin, when the storms come, when we feel disoriented or exhausted—we seek others so as to not be alone. Psalm 133 reminds us of the blessing that flows over us, refreshes us, and binds us together.

So, let's gather with our people. Let's stick together. Let's praise God for what He's done, for what He's doing, and for the gift of never having to face this life alone.

ABOUT PSALM 133

Psalm 133 is one of the Psalms of Ascent, hymns that God's people sang together as they made their pilgrimage to Jerusalem. These songs drew them closer to God and closer to one another. Can you picture the people of Israel streaming from every corner of the land to gather and worship in Jerusalem? They came from different tribes, different stories, yet together they formed a great crowd, singing and praising as one.

David captures this moment, exclaiming, "Behold, how good and pleasant it is when brothers dwell in unity!" (v. 1).

Oily Beard & Overflowing Blessing

David describes unity as "the precious oil on the head, running down on the beard, on the beard of Aaron" (v. 2). This image might seem strange at first, but it makes sense when you think about the role of oil to God's people. Oil was sacred, a blessing, an ordination.

In today's terms, imagine something extravagant—like a waterfall of the finest perfume.

Life-Giving, Like the Morning Dew

David also says, "It is like the dew of Hermon, which falls on the mountains of Zion" (v. 3). Picture the dry, cracked ground soaking up the gentle morning dew. In those parched places, the dew is life giving.

When you're disconnected, your heart can feel like that thirsty land—brittle, lifeless, and longing for renewal. True community, the kind that refreshes your soul, is a gift God gives to His people.

Life Everlasting

The psalm ends with a beautiful promise: "For there the LORD has commanded the blessing, life forevermore" (v. 3). God's blessing is constant and unwavering, stretching beyond time to offer life that never loses its power.

In John 17:20–23, Jesus prayed for you to experience unity with other believers and with the triune God. He knows how deeply we need one another. Through His sacrifice, He made a way for you to belong. His love holds you securely and eternally. You're part of a family bound together with Him and the Father by His grace. "I in them and You in Me, that they may become perfectly one, so that the world may know that You sent Me and loved them even as You loved Me" (John 17:23).

Forever Seen, Forever Connected

So, what now? Maybe your disconnection feels like standing in a crowded room where no one sees you. Even in that loneliness, God's love calls out to you. He draws you back into His family, where you're known, valued, and loved.

DISCUSS PSALM 133

1. Think about a time when you've been disconnected from a group of friends, from colleagues, from your family, or from God. What words can you use to describe this feeling?

2. When you feel disconnected, God's Word and Sacraments can remind you of your Baptism into God's family and your identity in Christ. Write a prayer asking God to help you remember this.

PRAY

Dear Lord, when I feel disconnected from You and others, remind me of the joy and power found in praising Your name together with others. Help me to come before You with an open heart, ready to experience Your presence and renew my spirit. May my worship unite me with others in love and strengthen our faith. Amen.

Lament Psalms

How long, O LORD? Will You forget me forever? How long will You hide Your face from me? Psalm 13:1

Here's what I've noticed as I get older: Happy songs easily stick in my head. They change my mood, lift my spirits, and make life feel lighter. But my favorite songs? The sad ones. The songs that put to words truths that are almost too painful to speak aloud. They can make that raw emotion beautiful by wrapping it in just the right melody and mournful chords.

Why do we love sad songs? Because they're real. They speak to the struggles we all face—the hurt we carry, the shame that haunts us, the confusion of hard days, and the frustration of feeling stuck or overwhelmed. But even in the pain, there's a glimmer of hope woven into such songs.

The Lament Psalms are like that. They acknowledge the situation for what it is then invite us to bring everything to God—our fear, anger, shame, exhaustion, and doubt. The Lament Psalms are short, honest prayers. They are also long, tearful cries. Whatever we have, God welcomes it. He meets us in our mess and, with incredible grace, turns it into something beautiful.

A Clean Heart (Psalm 51)

Psalm 51 speaks directly to the feeling of shame. David's words in this psalm show us that God's grace is bigger than our shame. We can lay our failures at God's feet and trust that His mercy covers us. David writes, "Create in me a clean heart, O God, and renew a right spirit within me" (v. 10). These are the words of forgiveness through Christ.

In God I Trust (Psalm 56)

In Psalm 56, we lament what it feels like when life is confusing. In these moments, what's your next step? "When I am afraid, I put my trust in You" (v. 3). In the middle of any confusion, trust that God is still guiding you.

Peace. Sleep. Safe. (Psalm 4)

When you're carrying too many responsibilities, facing too many struggles, or just worn down by life, turn to Psalm 4 for comfort: "In peace I will both lie down and sleep; for You alone, O LORD, make me dwell in safety" (v. 8). This psalm is a reminder that when you're running on empty, God is your refuge.

Hold on to Hope (Psalm 126)

This psalm was written after a long season of hardship, but it's full of hope for what's to come: "Those who sow in tears shall reap with shouts of joy!" (v. 5). God is at work, bringing about restoration and joy. Hope is rooted in the truth that God is faithful.

Regret and Restoration (Psalm 38)

David describes his regret in this psalm: "My iniquities have gone over my head; like a heavy burden, they are too heavy for me" (v. 4). Even as he feels the impact of his choices, David trusts that God's compassion lasts and that He welcomes us back with mercy and grace, which gives us hope.

You Are My Refuge (Psalm 61)

Listen to this imagery in Psalm 61: "From the end of the earth I call to You when my heart is faint. Lead me to the rock that is higher than I" (v. 2). When life feels like too much to handle, this psalm reminds us that God is the Rock to lean on. He's the place we run to when we need peace. "For You have been my refuge, a strong tower against the enemy" (v. 3) and "let me take refuge under the shelter of Your wings!" (v. 4).

Praise the Lord! (Psalm 22)

Psalm 22 calls us to have faith when we're anguished. "My God, my God, why have You forsaken me?" (v. 1)—these are words of deep pain, words that Jesus Himself spoke from the cross. This psalm does not end in despair though. It acknowledges God's gracious rescue and expresses our hope in His deliverance: "You have rescued me from the horns of the wild oxen!" (v. 21). "He has not hidden His face from him, but has heard, when he cried to Him" (v. 24).

We Sat and Wept (Psalm 137)

Psalm 137 expresses the deep ache of nostalgia: "By the waters of Babylon, there we sat down and wept, when we remembered Zion" (v. 1). This psalm reminds us that God's love lasts through every season of life, guiding us forward even as we let go of the past.

Write Your Own Lament Psalm

A Lament Psalm gives you permission to bring your aches into God's light and to pour out your pain, sorrow, and longing. He's waiting to hold it all with you.

1. Start with the pain you can't carry alone.

What has become too heavy to hold? Is it grief, loss, frustration, or disappointment? Begin with the weight you feel right now. Imagine yourself with a friend who sees every wound. God is here, listening with compassion and tenderness.

2. Put words to the depth of your sorrow.

Try to describe this pain, no matter how dark it seems. Maybe it feels like you're in a wilderness, searching but not finding a way out, or it feels like waves of sorrow that won't allow you a moment to breathe. Include here images that capture how deeply you feel this. Lament is your way of calling out to be seen and known, to bring what's hidden into God's light.

3. Ask the hard questions.

Are there things you don't understand, times when and places where you feel abandoned or unheard? Speak these questions out loud. Verbalize the ones you don't want to admit. What do you long for God to explain? Lament Psalms make room for questions that have no answers. God's love invites you to bring these mysteries and frustrations to Him.

4. Remember who God has been.

Hold on to the things you know about God's heart. Maybe His kindness has steadied you in the past or His faithfulness felt like a rock when you needed it. Recall these glimpses of His character, the truth that hasn't changed. Lament reaches for the certainty that God is still near, even in silence. Let these truths anchor you, like stars that appear only in the darkest night.

5. Close with a fragile hope.

End with whatever hope you can find. Trust that God is here, carrying you through every shadowed valley. A Lament Psalm often leaves room for the "not yet," the space between pain and healing. God is with you, holding on to you with love that never lets go.

9. ASHAMED

Pride Comes Before the Fall

For Kenny, Theron, Bret, and Lee; thank you for loving us through this.

Psalm 51

1Have mercy on me, O God,
according to Your steadfast love;
according to Your abundant mercy
blot out my transgressions.
2Wash me thoroughly from my iniquity,
and cleanse me from my sin!

3For I know my transgressions,
and my sin is ever before me.
4Against You, You only, have I sinned
and done what is evil in Your sight,
so that You may be justified in Your words
and blameless in Your judgment.
5Behold, I was brought forth in iniquity,
and in sin did my mother conceive me.
6Behold, You delight in truth in the inward being,
and You teach me wisdom in the secret heart.

7Purge me with hyssop, and I shall be clean;
wash me, and I shall be whiter than snow.
8Let me hear joy and gladness;
let the bones that You have broken rejoice.

9 Hide Your face from my sins,
    and blot out all my iniquities.
10 Create in me a clean heart, O God,
    and renew a right spirit within me.
11 Cast me not away from Your presence,
    and take not Your Holy Spirit from me.
12 Restore to me the joy of Your salvation,
    and uphold me with a willing spirit.

13 Then I will teach transgressors Your ways,
    and sinners will return to You.
14 Deliver me from bloodguiltiness, O God,
    O God of my salvation,
    and my tongue will sing aloud of Your righteousness.
15 O Lord, open my lips,
    and my mouth will declare Your praise.
16 For You will not delight in sacrifice, or I would give it;
    You will not be pleased with a burnt offering.
17 The sacrifices of God are a broken spirit;
    a broken and contrite heart, O God, You will not despise.

18 Do good to Zion in Your good pleasure;
    build up the walls of Jerusalem;
19 then will You delight in right sacrifices,
    in burnt offerings and whole burnt offerings;
    then bulls will be offered on Your altar.

Parenting is a humbling journey full of mistakes, and our journeys were no exception. We were too strict with our daughter, even though she already put immense pressure on herself. We were too lenient with our son, who thrived with clear boundaries. We were hyperfocused on our daughter, who openly admitted she idolized our approval, while we stayed too distracted with our son, who needed constant interaction. We tried so hard to get it right, yet our efforts often fell short.

Eventually, all this caught up with us. We made some mistakes that embarrassed us and left us feeling exposed. Our Christian community shunned us. We felt so alone and so hurt by those who didn't seem to care.

The shame of this whole season was overwhelming, and our pride as parents took a major hit. Instead of leaning into honesty and seeking support, we did what many do in times of fear and humiliation: We hid. We pulled away from those who loved us, burdened by the sense that we'd failed and the uncertainty of how to move forward.

It was our pride that made this shame cut so deep. We had wanted to be good parents, to do everything right. But the pressure we placed on ourselves backfired. Like David, whose pride led him to make devastating choices with Bathsheba, choices that spiraled into even greater sins, we had let our need to be perfect blind us. When David was confronted with his own sin, he felt the crushing weight of shame. It was shame that drove my family to isolation, convincing us that we had to hide from everyone, just because a few were criticizing us.

David describes the burden of hiding his sin in Psalm 32. He writes about how keeping his struggles in the dark sapped his strength and left him broken. That's exactly how we felt. Our shame became a heavy cloud, distorting our perspective and keeping us from reaching out for help. We pulled away from people who might have loved and supported us if we'd been honest. Instead, we let our fear of judgment—and our wounded pride—push us deeper into loneliness.

But here's the truth we discovered: Only God can break through that fog of pride and shame. Only God offers perfect, unconditional love. His forgiveness, through Jesus, washes over us, releasing us from the need to hide. As David eventually realized and expressed in Psalm 32:5–7, confession brings healing. Tell God your sin, receive His forgiveness, be found and be seen, depend on God to nourish you as you tuck yourself into His perfect care.

This was the painful but necessary lesson we learned. God's grace doesn't merely cover our mistakes; it redeems them. Even when our pride made us cling to our own broken ways, God's love never wavered. We had to humble ourselves, acknowledge our imperfections, and trust that God would make something beautiful from our failures.

Living through that season was messy and exhausting. Our family craved control of the circumstances, but God wanted us to surrender ourselves to Him. We were made for communion with Christ and honest, vulnerable relationships with others.

The pain of that season will eventually fade, but the lessons will remain. We will still struggle, still stumble, but I pray we remember what David learned: Shame isolates, but God's grace draws us close. We are God's children, forgiven and loved. Let's run to the cross, accept Christ's forgiveness, and live humbly and honestly with our community.

ABOUT PSALM 51

Raw, Honest Redemption

Psalm 51 is a raw expression of what it feels like to be weighed down by shame. Yet, it's also a beautiful reminder of how God's forgiveness meets us right in our brokenness. When David wrote this psalm, he was at one of his darkest moments. He had committed adultery with Bathsheba and arranged for her husband, Uriah, to be killed in battle to cover up his sin. David's pride made him feel untouchable. His sin left him devastated, overwhelmed with guilt and the crushing realization of how he had strayed from God.

No Hiding—Only Seeking

Instead of trying to hide, David came to God and admitted his mistakes. He owned up to his sin with complete honesty. His shame was heavy, affecting every part of his life. His spirit felt crushed, his heart burdened. Psalm 51 shows us that even when we're drowning in shame, God never gives up on us. No matter what we've done, His love lasts forever.

Create in Me

One of the most important moments in Psalm 51 comes when David says, "Create in me a clean heart, O God, and renew a right spirit within me" (v. 10). The word translated as "create" here is the same Hebrew word used in Genesis for when God created the world. This is divine creating that only God can do. David's sin had left his heart filthy and beyond his repair, but he believed in God's power to make something entirely new. This is grace in Jesus Christ—taking what is broken, sinful, and unclean and redeeming it.

A Clean Heart

In ancient Israel, Psalm 51 was often recited during times of repentance, like the Day of Atonement when the people laid their sins before God and asked for His forgiveness. It was a collective way of acknowledging, "We've messed up, but we trust You to restore us."

David's words resonate deeply because we, too, know what it feels like to be haunted by our shame. What's remarkable is that God's love is based on His character—His desire to redeem us—rather than any merit of our own.

The Joy of Your Salvation

David's prayer doesn't stop at forgiveness; he longs to feel joy again. "Restore to me the joy of Your salvation, and uphold me with a willing spirit" (v. 12). Shame will rob you of your joy, making you feel disconnected from God and from others. It eats away at your sense of worth. But God doesn't just forgive us; He sent His Son, Jesus, to restore us. That restoration, that salvation, is the joy we pray for.

Truly Clean, Truly Forgiven

Jesus took all our shame and guilt upon Himself, offering us the chance to be truly clean through His righteousness. Because of His sacrifice, we don't have to carry our pride and shame anymore. Jesus washed it all away.

DISCUSS PSALM 51

1. As humans, the weight of shame can become part of our identities. When have you experienced this in your own life?

2. Reflect on the relief in David's words in Psalm 51. How does this psalm's message of forgiveness and renewal speak to you today?

PRAY

Jesus, my Savior, when shame feels heavy on my heart, remind me of Your sacrifice and endless grace. Help me come to You with honesty and humility, trusting in Your readiness to forgive and restore. Renew my spirit, fill me with Your joy, and let me rest in Your boundless love. In Your precious name. Amen.

10. CONFUSED

The Case of the Missing Identity in Terminal B

For Sam, the hero of this story, whose encouragement and speed often save the day.

Psalm 56

1 Be gracious to me, O God, for man tramples on me;
all day long an attacker oppresses me;
2 my enemies trample on me all day long,
for many attack me proudly.
3 When I am afraid,
I put my trust in You.
4 In God, whose word I praise,
in God I trust; I shall not be afraid.
What can flesh do to me?

5 All day long they injure my cause;
all their thoughts are against me for evil.
6 They stir up strife, they lurk;
they watch my steps,
as they have waited for my life.
7 For their crime will they escape?
In wrath cast down the peoples, O God!

8 You have kept count of my tossings;
put my tears in Your bottle.
Are they not in Your book?

9 Then my enemies will turn back
in the day when I call.
This I know, that God is for me.
10 In God, whose word I praise,
in the LORD, whose word I praise,
11 in God I trust; I shall not be afraid.
What can man do to me?

12 I must perform my vows to You, O God;
I will render thank offerings to You.
13 For You have delivered my soul from death,
yes, my feet from falling,
that I may walk before God
in the light of life.

Losing your ID before a flight is a nightmare scenario I don't recommend. Here's what happened when it became my experience at one of the busiest airports in the world.

Our family trip to New York City had been a bucket-list adventure, filled with miles of walking and snapshots of famous landmarks. But when I look back on our pictures, I barely remember the sights. Instead, I think about the brain fog I was suffering from at the time, caused by long COVID. My mind was slow, like a foggy, seasick haze that made even simple thoughts feel heavy. If you've suffered from brain fog, you know what I mean. It's like a six-hundred-pound weight pressing down on your ability to think.

This fog followed me into the crowded LaGuardia airport. As our family finally reached the TSA agent after waiting in line for two grueling hours, I realized I didn't have my ID. Cold panic washed over me. Mike and the kids were already past the TSA agent and moving to security, but I was stuck. Loud static filled the space where I needed clear thoughts about where I had left my purse.

"If you don't have ID, get out of line," the TSA agent barked, her voice cutting through my panic. Tears welled up. I couldn't swallow.

Mike stared at me, his eyes wide with fear and frustration. This felt manageable until I saw my dread mirrored in his face.

I fumbled through my backpack, hoping I'd just overlooked it. The TSA agent grew impatient, yelling for me to move aside. The travelers behind me had their own airport dramas and had no patience for mine.

What happened next felt like a frantic blur, as if I were watching from underwater. Mike helped the kids through security while pleading with the TSA agents to help me prove my identity without an ID. They pushed him along through security, telling him not to slow down the line.

On the other side of security, Catie called me and tried to help me think of where I had left my purse. Was it on the ferry to Brooklyn? At the deli where we'd had lunch? In the Uber? The other kids scrolled through the photos they'd taken throughout the day, trying to piece together a timeline of when I'd last had my purse.

I ran to the bathroom we had used when we first arrived, all while fielding texts from Mike, who was getting nowhere with the TSA agents. "Everyone says you'll have to book another flight," he texted. "Thousands of dollars, no guarantee when you'll fly out."

Panic pulsed through my body, but my brain was a blank void. Then, progress. Catie remembered she had taken a screenshot of our Uber driver's profile. She'd saved it as a joke, thinking the ride deserved a spot on her Snapchat story. That screenshot had his phone number, and she started calling him.

I felt completely defeated. Then Mike texted what felt like my last hope. He explained the plan in simple, patient words, as if speaking to a scared child: "Go to the TSA office. It's an unmarked room next to security. Ask for Rhonda. She will help you."

As I dragged my luggage, my Apple Watch pinged with flight alerts. Twenty minutes. Fifteen. Ten. I finally found the unmarked TSA office, and Rhonda appeared, a stern woman who looked like she hadn't bent a rule in her life. My voice cracked as I explained my situation.

"You are a sad mess," Rhonda said.

"Yes," I agreed.

"I'm going to ask you some questions to prove you are who you say you are," she announced. "Former names? Other addresses? Describe a government building near your address. What color is the closest school?"

None of this made sense. Where is my post office? My brain conjured a completely unhelpful image of a post office in Galveston where I learned to parallel park. Rhonda shook her head, skeptical.

"Where do your kids go to school?" she pressed. I told her the name, but when I tried to explain it was a private Christian school, she looked more exasperated.

"I'm sorry," I said. "I'm scared. I can't think straight."

"Boarding now," Mike texted. "We won't have our phones in a minute. You'll be on your own."

I was failing. The terror must have shown on my face, because Rhonda did the wildest thing. "I'm going to let you through," she said.

Everything happened in a rush. Rhonda shepherded me through side doors, past staring travelers. I quickly texted Mike, "Getting through! Tell them to wait!" Sam appeared, grabbed my bags, and sprinted toward the gate, shouting for me to follow.

Mike was waiting outside the Jetway, pleading with the gate agent, who was visibly fed up. "RUN," he shouted. Nate and Elisabeth were yelling encouragement, but I barely registered it. My body was numb as I stumbled down the Jetway.

As I made my way down the airplane aisle, other passengers glared at me, angry at the delay. My kids cheered. Relief spilling over, I collapsed into my seat.

Later, when the adrenaline settled, I opened my phone. There were messages from my parents and from friends who we had asked to pray.

And one from the Uber driver: He had found my purse and was mailing it to me at his own expense. "I'm sorry for your stress," he wrote. His note ended with "I'll pray for you."

Confusion is as old as humanity. Illness, bewildering circumstances, or spiritual attacks can make everything feel scrambled. David knew this feeling. In Psalm 56, he wrote about his enemies closing in, the terror of feeling surrounded and powerless. Sometimes, those enemies are outside forces. Sometimes, they're ourselves.

Even when everything else fails—my plans, my memory, my strength—God remains steadfast. Even when I am confused, He is not. God is still God. He still loves me and helps me. He sees my weakness and still has compassion. He hears my prayers and responds with His mercy.

And that is never confusing.

ABOUT PSALM 56

David wrote Psalm 56 while he was held captive by the Philistines. His prayer holds the uncertainty he felt about his situation. It's a feeling we know well—when nothing makes sense and we don't know our next step. But David, even in the middle of his confusion, is certain about his faith in God.

Crushed but Trusting

After lamenting this feeling, David makes this shift: "When I am afraid, I put my trust in You" (v. 3). His fear does not disappear, but he leans into God's love.

This is the heart of Psalm 56. David reminds himself—and us—that God is trustworthy. He says, "In God, whose word I praise, in God I trust; I shall not be afraid" (v. 4). It's like David is saying, "I don't have to have everything figured out because I know that God's got me."

Tears in a Bottle

Historically, people have prayed Psalm 56 when they feel surrounded or struggle with what to do next. One of the most comforting lines in the psalm is, "You have kept count of my tossings; put my tears in Your bottle" (v. 8). God knows every tear, every restless night when we tossed and turned, every moment of confusion.

Trampled

Jesus walked through chaotic moments of human pain. We see Him experience these in the Garden of Gethsemane and then on the cross. But even in those moments, He trusted His Father's love. He took the next step. He obeyed what He had come to do. On the cross, He carried the full burden of our fear and uncertainty, ensuring that we are never alone in our confusion.

If you feel confused, let Psalm 56 remind you that God's love is steady and constant. He is collecting every tear, guiding you through every step, and reminding you that His love lasts forever, even in the confusion.

DISCUSS PSALM 56

1. Talk about what confusion feels like to you. What are the lingering effects of times when you've been confused?

2. How has God provided in your moments of confusion? What helps you trust Him when you feel disoriented?

PRAY

Father, in my moments of confusion and uncertainty, I turn to You as my refuge and strength. Help me to trust in Your wisdom and guidance, knowing You hear my prayers and understand my struggles. Grant me clarity of mind and peace of heart as I lean on Your promises. In Your Son's name. Amen.

11. EXHAUSTED

Rage Against the Machines

For Mom, who always reminds me to rest.

Psalm 4

1 Answer me when I call, O God of my righteousness!
You have given me relief when I was in distress.
Be gracious to me and hear my prayer!

2 O men, how long shall my honor be turned into shame?
How long will you love vain words and seek after lies? *Selah*
3 But know that the LORD has set apart the godly for Himself;
the LORD hears when I call to Him.

4 Be angry, and do not sin;
ponder in your own hearts on your beds, and be silent. *Selah*
5 Offer right sacrifices,
and put your trust in the LORD.

6 There are many who say, "Who will show us some good?
Lift up the light of Your face upon us, O LORD!"
7 You have put more joy in my heart
than they have when their grain and wine abound.

8 In peace I will both lie down and sleep;
for You alone, O LORD, make me dwell in safety.

The bad news is you are not a machine.

The good news is you are not a machine.

This past month, I felt like I was running on autopilot. With several speaking events lined up for teenagers and their parents, I found myself becoming more efficient with every engagement. Waking up early, staying up late, grinding through every single task—I was in the zone, checking off accomplishments like clockwork and feeling oddly proud of how productive I had become.

Then, all of that changed when I went to the mountains to speak to a hundred women, most of them in their seventies and eighties. These women had a completely different rhythm to their lives. They hadn't seen the TikToks preaching the gospel of grind culture, and they didn't believe the lie that our value is in what we do. They had stopped caring about compromising themselves to keep everyone happy. I watched them and immediately noticed the difference in their slower pace, their different priorities, their authenticity.

These women knew the futility of striving for more, more, more. They had learned the hard way that trying to earn approval only leads to frustration. Long ago, they had stopped trying to keep all the plates spinning and now their joy was in long meals with friends and family.

Instead of pushing themselves endlessly, they modeled what it looked like to embrace doing less. They lingered over conversations I would have rushed through. They savored the sleep I had denied myself. They accepted their weaknesses rather than punishing themselves to overcome them. They understood the need for real relief and a peace that surpasses understanding. They knew how to trust God for their true joy.

In other words, they saw God as powerful and themselves as human.

I, on the other hand, do not like the fragile, human parts of myself. I resent my body when it doesn't perform. I walk through my day irritated at my own limits, convinced I should push harder. Rest feels like something I must earn, a reward for completing everything on my to-do list.

Give me one hundred milligrams of caffeine, loud music through my AirPods, and solitude. Give me curated Instagram Reels with fifteen seconds of wisdom, transformations, and tutorials—an endless stream if I need them.

But please, don't remind me of my limits. Don't tell me that joy doesn't come from approval or accomplishments. Don't give me hurt feelings, broken promises, or traffic jams. Don't make me face the truth that everything human eventually lets us down.

Do you feel this way, like you can't afford to slow down?

At this convention, as I watched these older women, I saw that they understood something I didn't. In our conversations, I heard their wisdom. They knew that we are not machines. Even more important, we're not gods. We're human. We need help. We need peace. We need to slow down and remember that we were created to need the sweet relief that only our Savior can provide.

In a world that tells us to keep going, Psalm 4 gives us permission to stop. It reminds us that rest is not just a nice idea; it's essential. True rest—the kind that lets you lie down and sleep—doesn't come from your productivity but from placing your trust in God.

That weekend in the mountains, Psalm 4 spoke to me in a new way. God wasn't asking for my perfection; He was offering me the rest I had stubbornly refused. I realized that I didn't have to grind myself down to be worthy. He was reminding me that, in Him, there is something better than perfection. There is peace. There is hope. There is strength to keep going because we've learned to trust the one who sustains us.

ABOUT PSALM 4

God Gives Relief

Are you running on empty? Read David's description about how it feels to be completely drained and in need of divine rest. He writes in verse 1, "Answer me when I call, O God of my righteousness! You have given me relief when I was in distress." I love David's faith that God will give him relief from his exhaustion.

God Gives Comfort

When you're exhausted, it feels like you're responsible for everything. You push yourself harder, believing that when you improve, life will improve. In verses 3 and 4, David rests in the promise that his life belongs to the Lord.

God Gives Rest

David wrote this psalm as he struggled as king. He couldn't make everyone happy, and trying was wearing him out. In his fatigue, he turned to the source of true rest—God's love. In verse 8, he gives this comforting statement: "In peace I will both lie down and sleep; for You alone, O LORD, make me dwell in safety."

God Gives Peace

Throughout history, Psalm 4 has been used as an evening prayer, a way to unwind and trust God with the stresses of the day. God offers this same peace to you, even in our hectic modern world. Bring your frustration to your Father. He will put joy in your heart (verse 7), and you will dwell in His safety (verse 8).

God Gives Faith

Psalm 4 shows the idea of *sola fide* (faith alone). David's confidence is not in his own strength but in God's righteousness. It is your faith that gives you satisfaction, not your accomplishments. Remember this when you're tempted to be a people-pleaser. Because as David learned, and as so many exhausted people will tell you, that effort will wear you out.

Peace from Our Savior

Psalm 4 beautifully points us to Jesus as the one who offers true rest. When David cries out to God for safety, he's praying for a peace that goes beyond what this world can give. Jesus fulfills this need perfectly. He tells us, "Peace I leave with you; My peace I give to you. Not as the world gives do I give to you" (John 14:27).

Take Psalm 4 as an invitation to pause. Breathe. Remember you can rest. God's love is safe, and it endures with a strength that lasts forever.

DISCUSS PSALM 4

1. What parts of your life right now exhaust you? Does your work feel like it never ends? What keeps you grinding away, feeling like you're not allowed to rest?

2. How can you reconnect with God's Word and Sacraments? What reminds you that the Lord is taking care of you?

PRAY

Father, Creator and Sustainer of life, exhaustion weighs heavy on me and I come to You seeking rest and renewal. Grant me Your peace that surpasses understanding and strength to endure. Help me to find refuge in Your presence and to trust in Your care for me. Refresh my spirit and restore my energy as I lean on You. In Jesus' name. Amen.

12. HOPEFUL

Walking One Million Miles—Together

For Jen, who shows up.

Psalm 126

1When the LORD restored the fortunes of Zion,
    we were like those who dream.
2Then our mouth was filled with laughter,
    and our tongue with shouts of joy;
then they said among the nations,
    "The LORD has done great things for them."
3The LORD has done great things for us;
    we are glad.

4Restore our fortunes, O LORD,
    like streams in the Negeb!
5Those who sow in tears
    shall reap with shouts of joy!
6He who goes out weeping,
    bearing the seed for sowing,
shall come home with shouts of joy,
bringing his sheaves with him.

I've walked about a million miles with Jen over the past thirty years. Our friendship was built during freezing walks in Seward, Nebraska, in the early 1990s. The single-digit temperatures didn't bother us much as we huddled together, trudging through gusting winds. We had started nightly walks to work off the biscuits and gravy from Brommer, but it was the conversation that kept us going—talking about meetups, breakups, classes, summer plans, and how to decorate our dorm rooms. More than once, we laughed so hard we had to stop to wipe away tears.

Our walks have always felt like both a physical and emotional journey that has carried us through the highs and lows of life. As we have grown older, our walks have changed with us. During student teaching in Springfield, Illinois, we walked in circles around the church parking lot, talking and talking to understand life.

One of our hardest walks happened when Jen was teaching in Fort Lauderdale. We talked about how my upcoming marriage would change our friendship, and the weight of that conversation hung heavy between us. But you know what? The action of putting one foot in front of the other made it easier to be honest. We were already physically uncomfortable; there was no harm in being emotionally uncomfortable too.

We kept walking through our twenties. Jen moved to Houston, married one of our best friends, and taught English with me at a Christian high school. These miles felt weightier than our college days. We were no longer discussing dorm room decorations and midterms; instead, we were fretting over our careers, finances, and where life would take us. On triple-digit Texas days, we'd keep our heads down, slogging through the heat, talking about the more painful parts of life. One summer day, while Jen was pet-sitting down the street from our townhouse, the dogs we were walking started to fight in the middle of our deep conversation. It felt like a physical manifestation of the internal battles we were facing—like a spiritual attack right in front of us.

From 2003 to 2010, I lived an hour away from Jen, and we both had children—seven babies between us. We met in malls and random parks, finding our way with MapQuest directions. Our walks were interrupted by crying babies and hungry toddlers in strollers. We carried emotional and literal loads, from the burden of sleepless nights to the weight of diaper bags and bottles. Those years were heavy in every way.

When our children were a little older, my family moved back near Jen, and our walks were more frequent. The topics were even deeper now—depression, heartbreak, frustration, awe. When words ran out, we walked in silence, letting our pace and distance speak. Moving forward physically helped us process emotionally.

So much has changed since 1992, and yet, in many ways, nothing has changed. We still get lost on walks, though now we don't have to call our husbands to rescue us. We still talk about everything, though now there are topics like packing our kids' cars for college.

Walking stretches the body in ways that sitting and talking never can. The rhythm of our steps and the effort of movement feel raw, hopeful, alive. Even when we think we don't have time or energy, we keep meeting for these walks. And I'm so glad we do.

Walking with Jen reminds me of Psalm 126, a Psalm of Ascent. The pilgrims who traveled to Jerusalem would sing songs like this as they climbed. Jerusalem was the highest city in the region, and their journey was an upward one, both physically and spiritually. Those sojourners were tired, hungry, and surely irritable, but they kept moving forward together. Brothers, sisters, friends journeying side by side and singing as they went. The rhythm and motion of ascending must have cleared away the fog of tedious, frustrating everyday life.

Walking with Jen always leaves me feeling hopeful. Even if we haven't solved all our problems, we've moved through them together. It reminds me that just like the pilgrims in the psalms, we don't walk this road alone. God is with us every step, leading us upward toward faith, toward a new vantage point, and toward hope. Our steady footsteps and forward motion remind me that, no matter what, the Lord's mercy, hope, and love go before us. They endure forever.

ABOUT PSALM 126

Psalm 126 is the believer's celebration that God provides hope. In verses 5–6, the psalmist writes, "Those who sow in tears shall reap with shouts of joy! He who goes out weeping, bearing the seed for sowing, shall come home with shouts of joy, bringing his sheaves with him." This is a hope that lasts forever and forever.

Hope in the Journey

For the pilgrims through history who have sung Psalm 126, the journey itself would have been hopeful. Think about it—they were walking toward Jerusalem, toward the temple, toward the presence of God. And as they walked, they reminded themselves of what God had done before, how He had restored their fortunes and filled their mouths with laughter. They were walking with memories of God's past faithfulness and with hope that He would do it again.

Streams in the Desert

Psalm 126 uses hopeful imagery. For example, "streams in the Negeb" (v. 4) refers to a very dry desert region. Just as the Negeb would see water and life only after the rain, the people trusted that God would bring life and joy after each season of drought and difficulty. The Israelites walked, knowing that the rains would come. In the same way, God's love would refresh their spirits.

Hope in Christ Alone

Finally, all this walking imagery points us to Christ, who walked the path to the cross out of perfect love for you and me. His journey, filled with pain and sacrifice, ended in the greatest hope of all—the resurrection and eternal life. Because of Him, we walk through our own seasons of difficulty with hope, knowing that God is with us now and forever.

Never, Ever Alone

Are you in a season where you're walking through hardship, feeling weary? Let Psalm 126 encourage you. You're not walking alone. Even if you're sowing tears right now, God is with you on the journey. He promises that those who go out weeping will return with songs of joy. Keep walking, keep trusting that God's love lasts forever and that He is leading you toward something He has only for you.

DISCUSS PSALM 126

1. Look at verses 4, 5, and 6. Which of these images have you experienced in your own life?

2. What are some ways you can sow seeds of faith and hope in your life and community, as described in Psalm 126?

PRAY

Lord, I feel overwhelmed by life's pain and confusion. Remind me of Your faithfulness and restore my hope. Remind me that You work all circumstances to Your glory. You fill my heart with hope that surpasses understanding. In Jesus' name. Amen.

13. REGRETFUL

On Broken Crosses

For Amy, thank you for taking such good care of every one of us.

Psalm 38

1 O LORD, rebuke me not in Your anger,
nor discipline me in Your wrath!
2 For Your arrows have sunk into me,
and Your hand has come down on me.

3 There is no soundness in my flesh
because of Your indignation;
there is no health in my bones
because of my sin.
4 For my iniquities have gone over my head;
like a heavy burden, they are too heavy for me.

5 My wounds stink and fester
because of my foolishness,
6 I am utterly bowed down and prostrate;
all the day I go about mourning.
7 For my sides are filled with burning,
and there is no soundness in my flesh.
8 I am feeble and crushed;
I groan because of the tumult of my heart.

9 O LORD, all my longing is before You;
my sighing is not hidden from You.

10 My heart throbs; my strength fails me,
and the light of my eyes—it also has gone from me.
11 My friends and companions stand aloof from my plague,
and my nearest kin stand far off.

12 Those who seek my life lay their snares;
those who seek my hurt speak of ruin
and meditate treachery all day long.

13 But I am like a deaf man; I do not hear,
like a mute man who does not open his mouth.
14 I have become like a man who does not hear,
and in whose mouth are no rebukes.

15 But for You, O LORD, do I wait;
it is You, O Lord my God, who will answer.
16 For I said, "Only let them not rejoice over me,
who boast against me when my foot slips!"

17 For I am ready to fall,
and my pain is ever before me.
18 I confess my iniquity;
I am sorry for my sin.
19 But my foes are vigorous, they are mighty,
and many are those who hate me wrongfully.
20 Those who render me evil for good
accuse me because I follow after good.
21 Do not forsake me, O LORD!
O my God, be not far from me!
22 Make haste to help me,
O Lord, my salvation!

Interstate 45 runs straight through our town of Houston, and it's always buzzing with traffic. I still cringe when I think about the day when three of my students at the Christian high school where I teach crossed it transporting a huge cross, which ended up shattered.

In my class, Articulating Your Faith, students are responsible for planning and leading a chapel service. This semester, I had ten juniors and seniors working together on this service. The chapel service they envisioned centered around a stunning, eight-foot-tall, three-hundred-pound wooden cross that my church, Gloria Dei, had let us borrow.

The message was based on John 15:5 and clinging to Christ, the Vine. The students set the cross on the stage and wrapped it in vines to create a striking visual centerpiece for their service.

The class divided into groups to lead chapel. Some kids had speaking parts. Others led the liturgy. Three boys had signed up to help transport the cross. They were supposed to pick it up the day before chapel and then return it the next afternoon. I had spoken to my pastor and he agreed to help us get the ginormous cross across town—no small feat.

When it came to transporting the cross from my church to our high school gym, only one student showed up to help, leaving my husband and me struggling to load the cross into our truck. On chapel day, I was already frustrated with other two boys who hadn't helped.

Despite the rough start, the service was beautiful. The students who had speaking parts shared their hearts about God's love. They had practiced, prayed, and spoken passionately. The cross stood as the focal point of their message, and I was so grateful for how it all came together.

After the service, the other students headed to class while I explained to the tear-down committee that we needed to return the cross to Gloria Dei immediately after school.

"Sorry, Mrs. Hergenrader. Spring football practice," one of them said.

"What about after that? It'll take thirty minutes. Tops."

"No can do," they argued.

"It's a major grade," I pointed out.

"We'll just have to fail," they said.

"If you fail this, you will fail the class."

"Wait. I have an idea," one of the boys said with a grin. "We'll drive the cross back to the church now." The others lit up immediately. "I've got my truck right there," he said, pulling out his keys.

I was shaking my head because it was a terrible idea. "You can't leave during the day, you don't have your parents' permission to ride together, you don't even know where you're going, and you would have to cross I-45."

These arguments inspired them. They were now lawyers giving their closing arguments, using my own list of class requirements against me. "We don't want to fail a major project. We can't possibly do our part in any other way, except by missing the next hour of class for this very important errand. This is the only time we could possibly go."

"This is the worst idea I've ever heard," I said. Yet, a part of my brain was already starting to cave. The situation had worn me out. I knew, and these boys knew, it was a trade. I gave permission for them to miss school and they took something off my to-do list.

"Come on, Mrs. Hergenrader. We promise. It's good. We will be so careful."

I was shaking my head even as I was agreeing. If they left right now, the whole thing would be done in a half hour. Even as I told them the idea broke one hundred rules, they were pulling out their phones and texting their parents for permission. And I was letting them.

The next few minutes were a flurry of the boys making plans, based loosely on ideas that were not totally accurate. With their parents' permission, could they legally leave school? I didn't know, but they were shouting, "Yes! Of course, we can. We do it all the time!" Could they ride with each other? Doesn't Texas have a law against minors driving nonfamily members? "That's not a thing. We drive together all the time!" Did they know the way to the church? "What? Yes!"

This is where I have to mention that I knew, without a doubt, that none of these statements were true. They were telling me they knew how to get to the church at the same moment they were googling directions. One of them was texting furiously, trying to get his reluctant mom's permission. And Texas definitely has a law against kids under age 18 driving together (I have teenagers, so I know this).

I was getting snowed—and I knew I was letting myself get snowed. It wasn't legal or even safe for the boys, but it would keep me safe from uncomfortable feelings of being angry with them.

As I was stuffing down those uncomfortable feelings and telling myself lame excuses about the dangers, two of the boys were already hauling the cross to the waiting truck. Then, another faculty member came over to see what was happening.

There is something about men and trucks and rope. Because without even discussing the actual process or idea, they began tying down the cross and talking about knots and balance and strategic ways to make sure it stayed in the truck. Even though the adrenaline of THIS IS A TERRIBLE IDEA was pulsing through me, I stood silently and watched. I even texted Mike a picture and said, THIS IS A TERRIBLE IDEA.

It only took one second for him to view the picture and reply, "It's too heavy to be carried like that. It will fall out." But his text came through as the boys were already jumping into the cab and assuring me through the open window that they would be back "in just a minute!"

I told them, in my most stern teacher voice (that honestly had zero effect since they were doing whatever they wanted), that they must be very safe and they must go straight to the church and come back immediately. I held up my phone. "Text me when you get to Gloria Dei. I will stand exactly right here. If I don't hear from you in fifteen minutes, I will start calling you. Do you understand?"

Yes, yes, of course, they did. They were already driving away, the cross bouncing on the back of the truck.

You know what happened next. The cross, that big and beautiful (borrowed) symbol of faith, bounced out of the truck bed and onto the highway. Thankfully, no one was hurt, but the cross shattered, leaving pieces scattered across the lanes. The boys managed to pull over and, in their panic, retrieved the broken pieces.

Word spread quickly. A parent driving down I-45 saw the boys in their school uniforms and reported it to the school. Another administrator came outside to give me the news: The cross was now in pieces. All my hopes of keeping this errand low-key were gone.

When the boys made it back, they were visibly shaken. We stood there in the parking lot, me crying, them struggling to explain what had happened. The whole scene was a low point in my teaching career. My regret was overwhelming. I had failed to protect what was entrusted to me.

Psalm 38 captures this kind of remorse perfectly. David's words are full of anguish over his sins: "My wounds stink and fester because of my foolishness. . . . I am feeble and crushed; I groan because of the tumult of my heart" (vv. 5, 8). We may not relate to the specifics of David's sins, but we know how regret eats away at us. It affects our hearts and our minds, leaving us desperate for relief.

True relief comes through forgiveness.

I reconciled with these students. Looking them in the eye and apologizing for letting them do what I knew was wrong helped ease my guilt. I hope it helped them too. I love my students, and I hated the pain this incident caused all of us.

It's astounding how we justify what we want to do. We make choices we know are wrong, and the guilt and regret builds. Over time, it shapes how we see ourselves and others. We need God's grace to move on.

What regrets are you carrying? Maybe you've let something slide because confrontation felt too difficult. Maybe you've ignored your gut and got hurt as a result. Or maybe you've breached boundaries, knowing you were pushing too far but doing it anyway.

Like David, you can bring your regret to God. He offers forgiveness and reminds us that His love endures. We are new creations, and His grace wipes away our guilt, replacing it with the love of Christ. And we know this is true because faith is planted in our hearts.

ABOUT PSALM 38

Regret is heavy. It settles deep in your chest as a relentless reminder of things you wish you could undo. Look hard at your regret right now. Does it make you feel tense? Sad? Embarrassed? In physical pain?

Psalm 38 meets us right there, in the thick of that heaviness. David pours out his heart, giving voice to the kind of regret that so many of us carry but often struggle to express.

The Burden of Sin

David writes, "For my iniquities have gone over my head; like a heavy burden, they are too heavy for me" (v. 4). You may also feel this guilt that suffocates. His regret is palpable, almost physical, and isn't that so true to our lives too? When we let our mistakes fester, they seep into our very bones, draining our energy, constricting our chest.

Crying Out for God

But here's where David's story shifts. Even in the depths of his pain, he doesn't keep it to himself. He cries out, "But for You, O Lord, do I wait; it is You, O Lord my God, who will answer" (v. 15). There's a beautiful vulnerability in that. David's hope is in God—the only one who can truly heal him

The Promise of Grace

Jesus offers divine grace so beautifully in the Gospels. Time and again, He offers healing and forgiveness to those who feel burdened by their past. It's true that when we stop pretending and start being honest about our regret, we open ourselves up to God's transforming grace.

God's Steadfast Love

David closes the psalm with a desperate plea: "Do not forsake me, O LORD! O my God, be not far from me! Make haste to help me, O Lord, my salvation!" (vv. 21–22). Can you hear the urgency in his voice? Regret might feel overwhelming, but God's love surrounds us. It doesn't waver when we stumble. It doesn't shrink back when we mess up. Just the opposite. It pulls us closer, reminding us that we are loved and forgiven—not because we've earned it but because Jesus pursues us relentlessly, wraps us in His love, and embraces us with His forgiveness.

This is the love of our Savior, Jesus Christ.

DISCUSS PSALM 38

1. How does Psalm 38 help you process feelings of regret and guilt in your own life?

2. What steps can you take to experience the comfort and healing that come from God's presence and mercy as described in Psalm 38?

PRAY

Heavenly Father, Your grace is more than I can comprehend, and Your mercy never ends. I bring You my regrets, trusting You to lift the burden I carry. Forgive me when I hold on to guilt and let it eat away. Teach me to be honest with You, to lay everything at Your feet, and to rest in Your unshakable love. Guide me to live each day in Your grace. In Jesus' name. Amen.

14. OVERWHELMED

The Crying Era

For Jemma and Sophia, have the time of your life fighting dragons.

Psalm 61

1 Hear my cry, O God,
listen to my prayer;
2 from the end of the earth I call to You
when my heart is faint.
Lead me to the rock
that is higher than I,
3 for You have been my refuge,
a strong tower against the enemy.

4 Let me dwell in Your tent forever!
Let me take refuge under the shelter of Your wings! *Selah*
5 For You, O God, have heard my vows;
You have given me the heritage of those who fear Your name.

6 Prolong the life of the king;
may his years endure to all generations!
7 May he be enthroned forever before God;
appoint steadfast love and faithfulness to watch over him!

8 So will I ever sing praises to Your name,
as I perform my vows day after day.

If you have spent time around teenage girls recently, you know about Taylor Swift's Eras Tour. It's a Big. Deal. Outfit planning starts months in advance, favorite songs spark endless debates, and securing tickets can bring anxiety attacks. Beneath all the hype, though, there's something deeply moving about this tidal wave of emotion that goes far beyond the music.

It's the experience of being part of something larger. Tens of thousands of fans singing in unison, each voice contributing to a shared moment. You might see someone across the crowd, someone who doesn't look anything like you but who knows every word, singing with as much heart as you are. In that moment, it feels like all your differences dissolve. The effect of this shared experience is that girls cry and cry at her concerts.

But this experience of being overwhelmed isn't confined to pop star concerts. We all experience emotions that are so overwhelming that we lose it. And I've learned that we should pay attention to our tears.

It's those times when you watch your child experience something beautiful and you realize how fleeting this moment is. It's the ache of remembering someone you miss, the gratitude that wells up when surrounded by people you love, or the pain of being betrayed. Those feelings can be a lot—sometimes, more than we can handle. So we cry. Often, we don't want to *feel* this much because it makes us appear weak. Because it makes us too exposed and vulnerable. Because it makes us lose control. And we hate that.

But what if we accepted these overwhelming emotions as something good?

This sense of being emotionally flooded isn't new. It's part of being human, something the psalmists knew intimately. They captured a full spectrum of overwhelming feelings. In Psalm 55, the psalmist describes a heart so full of anxiety and fear that he says, "My heart is in anguish within me; the terrors of death have fallen upon me. Fear and trembling come upon me, and horror overwhelms me" (vv. 4–5).

Other times, the psalmists wrote about overwhelming joy. In Psalm 126, the writer reflected on a time when God restored His people: "Then our mouth was filled with laughter, and our tongue with shouts of joy" (v. 2). David speaks of tears that "have been my food day and night" (Psalm 42:3), showing how sorrow can consume us. In Psalm 6:6, he confesses, "I flood my bed with tears; I drench my couch with my weeping," a vivid picture of deep, raw anguish.

The Psalms remind us that being overwhelmed is part of being human, and God acknowledges it all. Jesus cried when He was moved by grief. He felt compassion for others so deeply that He acted to help them. He worked miracles to heal them, restore them to mortal life, and give them eternal life. Jesus knows what it's like to feel emotions that are bigger than words.

So, let yourself cry and cry. Laugh hard when joy surprises you. Stand in awe when something beautiful takes your breath away. Let your heart be overwhelmed by life's experiences. Through the Holy Spirit, you can take your overwhelming feelings to God in prayer, even when you don't have the words. In the middle of it all, God is there, steady and unwavering, holding you through every moment and offering comfort and strength.

ABOUT PSALM 61

Our emotions can be so overwhelming. In verse 2, David prays, "Lead me to the rock that is higher than I." His feelings make him wobbly, but he turns to God, who is steady, unshakable, and so much more powerful than anything we're feeling.

The Shelter of Your Wings

One of my favorite images is in verse 4: "Let me take refuge under the shelter of Your wings." The focus of this picture is the shelter of the protective wings, even if we often feel like needy, helpless birds. Our Father holds us close and protects us even as we feel crushing sadness, fragile joy, crippling anxiety, heartbreaking nostalgia.

Jesus echoed this same comfort when He lamented Jerusalem, saying, "How often would I have gathered your children together as a hen gathers her brood under her wings" (Matthew 23:37). Through His love, we are safe in God's everlasting care.

Unchanging Grace

There's a deep theological truth here: We are both fully human, with emotions that rise and fall, and fully forgiven by God, who washes away our sin. In the same way that we trust in God's grace to carry us through our sins, we trust Him heal our hearts and all that weighs us down. It's an act of faith to honestly confess our deepest feelings.

Come to Me

Through Jesus' life, death, and resurrection, we know that God's grace covers every part of us, even our overwhelming emotions. We find the much-needed rest in our Savior, who said, "As the Father has loved Me, so have I loved you. Abide in My love" (John 15:9).

DISCUSS PSALM 61

1. What overwhelms you? Talk about the parts of life that feel like too much.

2. Look at Psalm 61 again. Savor the rich wording to describe the feeling of being overwhelmed. What encourages you the most?

PRAY

Lord, when I feel overwhelmed by the pressures and struggles of life, help me to find my refuge in You. Strengthen me with Your peace and lead me to the safety of Your presence. Remind me of Your steadfast love and faithfulness and grant me the courage to trust in Your Word and in Your enduring love. In Jesus' name. Amen.

15. ANGUISHED

My Bones Are on Display

For Madeleine, who is fiercely brave.

Psalm 22

1 My God, my God, why have You forsaken me?
Why are You so far from saving me, from the words of my groaning?
2 O my God, I cry by day, but You do not answer,
and by night, but I find no rest.

3 Yet You are holy,
enthroned on the praises of Israel.
4 In You our fathers trusted;
they trusted, and You delivered them.
5 To You they cried and were rescued;
in You they trusted and were not put to shame.

6 But I am a worm and not a man,
scorned by mankind and despised by the people.
7 All who see me mock me;
they make mouths at me; they wag their heads;
8 "He trusts in the LORD; let Him deliver him;
let Him rescue him, for He delights in him!"

9 Yet You are He who took me from the womb;
You made me trust You at my mother's breasts.
10 On You was I cast from my birth,
and from my mother's womb You have been my God.

11 Be not far from me,
for trouble is near,
and there is none to help.

12 Many bulls encompass me;
strong bulls of Bashan surround me;
13 they open wide their mouths at me,
like a ravening and roaring lion.

14 I am poured out like water,
and all my bones are out of joint;
my heart is like wax;
it is melted within my breast;
15 my strength is dried up like a potsherd,
and my tongue sticks to my jaws;
You lay me in the dust of death.

16 For dogs encompass me;
a company of evildoers encircles me;
they have pierced my hands and feet—
17 I can count all my bones—
they stare and gloat over me;
18 they divide my garments among them,
and for my clothing they cast lots.

19 But You, O Lord, do not be far off!
O You my help, come quickly to my aid!
20 Deliver my soul from the sword,
my precious life from the power of the dog!
21 Save me from the mouth of the lion!
You have rescued me from the horns of the wild oxen!

22 I will tell of Your name to my brothers;
in the midst of the congregation I will praise You:
23 You who fear the Lord, praise Him!
All you offspring of Jacob, glorify Him,
and stand in awe of Him, all you offspring of Israel!
24 For He has not despised or abhorred
the affliction of the afflicted,

and He has not hidden His face from him,
    but has heard, when he cried to Him.

25 From You comes my praise in the great congregation;
    my vows I will perform before those who fear Him.
26 The afflicted shall eat and be satisfied;
    those who seek Him shall praise the LORD!
    May your hearts live forever!

27 All the ends of the earth shall remember
    and turn to the LORD,
and all the families of the nations
    shall worship before You.
28 For kingship belongs to the LORD,
    and He rules over the nations.

29 All the prosperous of the earth eat and worship;
    before Him shall bow all who go down to the dust,
    even the one who could not keep himself alive.
30 Posterity shall serve him;
    it shall be told of the Lord to the coming generation;
31 they shall come and proclaim His righteousness to a people yet unborn,
    that He has done it.

At our school, there's a tradition called the T-Time devotion, and it's a defining moment for my course, Articulating Your Faith. Each student stands in front of the entire high school—375 peers, teachers, and staff—and shares what God has done in their life. These devotions aren't about giving perfect speeches. They're about sharing real, honest stories. Stories of God's presence in the midst of their doubts, fears, and joys. Stories of how His love has carried them through hard times and shaped who they are.

It's incredible to watch. Teenagers, still figuring out who they are, stand up and speak with vulnerability and courage. For many, it's terrifying, but they do it anyway. And in those moments, they're doing something much bigger than they realize. They're trusting God to use their words—no matter how imperfect they might feel—to reach someone who needs to hear them.

When I watch my students, I can't help but think of David's words in Psalm 22. In the middle of his own fear and pain, David cried out to God with raw honesty, but he also declared God's faithfulness. My students are living that out. Their courage to share what God has done in their lives becomes a testimony to everyone in the room. Whether their classmates notice it now or later, these devotions plant seeds of hope and truth.

And isn't that a challenge for all of us? The students in Articulating Your Faith are stepping into something that makes me pause and reflect. How often do we hesitate to share what God has done in our lives? Whether it's with a friend, a family member, or someone who just needs a little encouragement, speaking about God's grace can feel intimidating. But just like these students, we're called to trust God to work in us and through us.

Psalm 22:30 says it beautifully: "Posterity shall serve Him; it shall be told of the Lord to the coming generation." These students aren't just speaking to their peers; they're speaking to something much larger. Their testimonies point to a God who has been faithful through every generation. And they inspire others—classmates, teachers, parents—to share that same Gospel story of hope.

This tradition is more than a class project or a rite of passage. It's a reminder that sharing what God has done in our lives *matters*. It matters today, for the people who hear it. It matters for the next generation, who will carry the story forward. And it matters for us, as we remember that God's faithfulness and love endure forever.

ABOUT PSALM 22

David's Cry

Psalm 22 begins with David's heart-wrenching question: "My God, my God, why have You forsaken me?" (v. 1). This cry stretches from his personal struggles to the trials of every person who has felt anguished. This is David's lament, and it's also the cry of all of Israel. Through their exile, hardships, and losses, God's people return to this lament over and over again.

Jesus & the Prophecy

When Jesus quotes this psalm from the cross, He embraces its message as His own (Matthew 27:46; Mark 15:34). Think about the significance of this moment. Jesus, God the Son, took on our human experience and shared our suffering so fully that He felt forsaken from His Father. In fact, God did abandon Him because that was the only way to pay for the sin of humanity, to fulfill the covenant. But because of that—because Jesus took that on for us—God will never abandon us. Never.

Psalm 22 prophesizes a mocked, scorned servant. His hands and feet are pierced, and His clothing is divided (vv. 7, 16, 18). This was no coincidence. Jesus understood the prophecy. He fully embraced it, and then He fulfilled it.

Trust Through Our Trials

When David remembers God's faithfulness in the past (vv. 3–5), he moves from a place of questioning to a place of trust.

Are there areas in your life where trust feels hard right now? What does your suffering feel like? Do you remember the times that God has been faithful? What is your response to that?

Bring Your Pain to God's Love

How can you bring your pain and worry and weakness to God today? Psalm 22 reminds you that every single one of us suffers. On this side of heaven, we will have agonizing moments. But God is righteous and is gracious and merciful beyond anything we can imagine. Even unto those generations yet to be born who will need to know about His everlasting love.

DISCUSS PSALM 22

1. What is agonizing to you? Is it public speaking? Is it facing a hard conversation? Is it something else? Describe the feeling of that suffering here.

2. Share a story of trusting that God was with you sometime in the past and how this strengthened your faith.

PRAY

Heavenly Father, I've suffered agonizing worry and loss in my life. In my fear, I focus on my pain rather than on Your plan. Please help me and remind me of Your faithfulness. Turn my worry to joy and my mourning to dancing. Provide for me, just as You provided the sacrifice of Your Son, Jesus. In His name. Amen.

16. NOSTALGIC

Exiled in California

To Kayla, Jennifer, Dave, Jesús, Nick, Christy, and Kari, to my Townsend Process Group; thank you for walking alongside me through this.

Psalm 137

1 By the waters of Babylon,
there we sat down and wept,
when we remembered Zion.
2 On the willows there
we hung up our lyres.
3 For there our captors
required of us songs,
and our tormentors, mirth, saying,
"Sing us one of the songs of Zion!"

4 How shall we sing the LORD's song
in a foreign land?
5 If I forget you, O Jerusalem,
let my right hand forget its skill!
6 Let my tongue stick to the roof of my mouth,
if I do not remember you,
if I do not set Jerusalem
above my highest joy!

7 Remember, O LORD, against the Edomites
the day of Jerusalem,

how they said, "Lay it bare, lay it bare,
    down to its foundations!"

8 O daughter of Babylon, doomed to be destroyed,
    blessed shall he be who repays you
    with what you have done to us!
9 Blessed shall he be who takes your little ones
    and dashes them against the rock!

I've always been struck by how many of us struggle to understand and express our emotions. We tuck them away, unsure how to unpack them or even acknowledge they're there. That realization made me want to help. I wanted to create a safe space where people could feel seen and understood, a place where their emotions were valued and explored. This calling led me to take a big step: enrolling in a life coaching program at the Townsend Institute in Irvine, California. It's a highly rated and challenging program, designed to teach people how to guide others toward healing and growth. But I knew I didn't want to do this alone; I wanted to share the journey.

So, I asked my friend Barb to join me. She and I have been through so much together over the last twenty years—celebrating birthdays, navigating heartbreaks, and sharing countless cups of coffee as we process the ups and downs of life. Together, we have felt a growing call to share Jesus' love in a deeper, more intentional way. So, with hearts full of anticipation, we enrolled in the program, unaware of just how transformative—and how challenging—the journey would be.

When we arrived in California, we were buzzing with excitement. But that energy soon turned to confusion as we pulled up to our Airbnb, a sprawling, maze-like apartment complex. Every hallway looked the same, weaving through identical corridors with identical door numbers. It seemed designed to disorient us, and we laughed at how ridiculous it felt as we dragged our suitcases through the endless halls and asked each other if we'd ever find the right door.

Then came the real work at the Townsend Institute. Each morning, we made our way to Concordia University, bracing ourselves for long, emotionally charged hours. The days were filled with process groups, where we shared our stories, pulled apart our memories, and unearthed feelings we hadn't looked at in years. It was like therapy boot camp: facing buried emotions, sitting with long-ignored pains, and learning to hold space for discomfort, all so we could do the same for others.

As I said, it was transformative. It was also incredibly hard. Have you ever tried to confront emotions you'd rather ignore? It's exhausting. Each session felt like peeling back layers to reveal griefs we hadn't processed, joys we'd been afraid to fully embrace, hurts we thought we'd outgrown. By evening, our minds were fried and our hearts felt heavy from the weight of it all.

Our retreat to the Airbnb became a ritual of its own, and that first night, even that felt impossible. The apartment complex was a literal maze. The weather mirrored how our hearts felt—lost, overwhelmed, and unsure which way to turn.

This is just like nostalgia, isn't it? It feels a lot like being caught in a maze. Nostalgia feels comforting at first, wrapping us in warm memories. But soon, we're caught in a loop, idealizing the past and struggling to move forward. Nostalgia can make us feel safe, but it can also trap us in memories that keep us from progressing.

Psalm 137 captures this perfectly. In Babylon, the exiled Israelites sat by the rivers and wept over their lost homeland: "By the waters of Babylon, there we sat down and wept, when we remembered Zion" (v. 1). To them in that moment, Jerusalem seemed idyllic, a place they longed to return to. But was it? Or had nostalgia clouded their memories, turning the past into something it never truly was?

The Israelites' memories of Jerusalem weren't entirely accurate. They remembered a flawless city but had forgotten the corruption and hardship that had been there too. Nostalgia made them mourn a past that, in reality, was just as layered and complicated as the present.

I get it. Nostalgia is one of those tricky emotions. It can be beautiful, yes, but it can cloud our vision. It leads us to mourn for what we've lost, even when that perfect past was a mix of highs and lows, joy and pain. Nostalgia can make us think that God's goodness is in the past, that what *was* is better than what *is* or what *could be*.

But Psalm 137 doesn't just dwell in longing. It takes a darker turn, shifting from nostalgia to bitterness—even vengeance. This shows how nostalgia, when unchecked, can steal our present joy and trap us in resentment.

Consider Lot's wife. She looked back and was turned into a pillar of salt (Genesis 19). It's a warning: clinging to the past can leave us frozen, unable to embrace God's blessings now. But God offers us a better way. "The steadfast love of the LORD never ceases; His mercies never come to an end; they are new every morning" (Lamentations 3:22–23). Each day brings fresh mercies, new reasons to trust Him, and a chance to let go. Jesus invites us to this same trust when He tells us, "behold, I am making all things new" (Revelation 21:5).

The more I learned at the Townsend Institute, the more I realized the benefits of untangling our emotions from nostalgia. Every season of life is a million things: joy and sorrow, growth and grief. When we let ourselves process those responses, we see that each season is rich with meaning, even if it's not perfect. Letting go of the past isn't about forgetting it; it's about finding freedom to fully live in the present and anticipate the future, to see God's mercies in every moment now and know that He has amazing things planned for us in eternity.

Eventually, Barb and I found our way back, soaked from a rainstorm and laughing at the absurdity of it all. Maybe that's the lesson: keep moving forward, even when we feel lost, and find the humor, grace, and beauty in the present—even when it's messy. Psalm 137 reminds us of the pain that comes with change, but it also warns us not to get stuck there. God calls us to trust Him with our future, to know that His love lasts, weaving through every season with new mercies every morning.

ABOUT PSALM 137

Psalm 137 is one of the most heartbreaking psalms, capturing the raw grief of the Israelites in exile. Imagine their devastation: Jerusalem, their beloved home, lay in ruins. The Babylonian Empire had conquered their city in 586 BC, destroying the temple and dragging them away to a foreign land.

Stripped of everything familiar, they felt lost, disoriented, and utterly disconnected from God. The psalm opens with a haunting image: "By the waters of Babylon, there we sat down and wept, when we remembered Zion" (v. 1). It wasn't just homesickness. It was a soul-deep mourning for the life they once knew, a longing for the presence of God they had felt so tangibly in their homeland.

How Can We Move Forward?

As you read, you feel their grief shift into something darker. Their longing turns to anger, even a desire for vengeance, as they try to process the pain of what's been taken from them. In verse 4, they cry out, "How shall we sing the LORD's song in a foreign land?" It's an honest question. How do you hold on to hope when everything has fallen apart? How do you keep faith when the bitterness of loss threatens to consume you? This psalm shows us something true and uncomfortable: Longing for a past we can't get back can cloud our vision, making it hard to see the beauty God is placing right in front of us.

Christ, Our Song in Exile

Psalm 137 also points us to a profound truth about Jesus. Just as the Israelites mourned their lost home, humanity grieves our lost place in God's paradise. Christ stepped into our broken world to bring us back to God. He understands our exile, our deep sense of separation. It's a call to trust Him, to release the past and believe that He is working in the present, guiding us toward a future filled with His promises. When we feel exiled, disconnected, or stuck, Jesus invites us to rest in Him, our true and eternal home.

DISCUSS PSALM 137

1. Have you ever found yourself longing for the past and feeling as though life will never be as good as it once was? How did that affect your ability to see the blessings of the present?
2. Have you noticed bitterness creeping into your heart because of unresolved hurt? What would it look like to bring those wounds to God and let Him replace them with peace?

PRAY

Lord, You know my heart and my longing. Help me let go of what's behind me and find peace in the present. Open my eyes to see Your new mercies today. Guide me forward with Your love. Amen.

Praise Psalms

I will give thanks to the LORD with my whole heart; I will recount all of Your wonderful deeds. Psalm 9:1

Life brings encounters with so many emotions—joy, grief, loneliness, even numbness—and sometimes, in the middle of all those feelings, we can forget the importance of praising God. The Praise Psalms remind us that, no matter what we're going through, God is always worthy of our praise. They show us that praising God isn't just something we do when we feel good—it's an act of faith that draws us closer to Him when life feels heavy.

Praising God lifts our eyes off our circumstances and fixes them on the one who never changes, who loves us deeply, and who walks with us through every moment. The Praise Psalms invite us to come as we are, to bring our loneliness, grief, and numbness as well as our joy and thankfulness and offer them to God in worship. These psalms reinforce for us His steadfast love and faithfulness.

Everlasting (Psalm 100)

Psalm 100 is a beautiful reminder that God loves you. Verse 5 shows the security of being fully known and fully loved. "For the LORD is good; His steadfast love endures forever, and His faithfulness to all generations."

When we feel loved by God, it changes everything—it grounds us, strengthens us, restores our hope, and gives us courage. Praise flows from the assurance that we are God's own, forever held in His love.

Whom Should I Fear? (Psalm 27)

Loneliness makes us feel isolated, like we're on the outside looking in, like the world is distant and scary. But Psalm 27 reminds us that God is always with us. "The LORD is my light and my salvation; whom shall I fear? The LORD is the stronghold of my life; of whom shall I be afraid?" (v. 1).

No matter how lonely we may feel, we are never truly alone. Verse 10 reminds us of this: "For my father and my mother have forsaken me, but the LORD will take me in." When loneliness presses in, voicing our praise reminds us that God is present with us in His Word.

Rejoice in Your Salvation (Psalm 13)

Psalm 13 offers words for your seasons of emotional numbness. "How long, O LORD? Will You forget me forever? How long will You hide Your face from me?" (v. 1).

Bring your heartache, your questions, and your weariness to God. He doesn't leave you to manage them on your own. Rather, His Spirit transforms your cries to rejoicing. "But I have trusted in Your steadfast love; my heart shall rejoice in Your salvation" (v. 5).

Where Does My Help Come From? (Psalm 121)

Psalm 121 is for when we're grieving. Grief can feel like an uphill climb, where we're weighed down by sorrow and it's hard to see the way forward. "I lift up my eyes to the hills. From where does my help come? My help comes from the LORD, who made heaven and earth" (vv. 1–2). This psalm reminds us that in our grief, God is our help. He is our strength and comforter, and the one who will carry us through the pain. "The LORD will keep you from all evil; He will keep your life" (v. 7). Expressing praise can feel hard when we are grieving, but the words of this psalm remind us that God is very much with us, guarding our hearts and giving us the grace to keep going.

Turn My Mourning to Dancing (Psalm 30)

Finally, Psalm 30 reminds us that joy can be found after seasons of sorrow. "You have turned for me my mourning into dancing; You have loosed my sackcloth and clothed me with gladness" (v. 11).

Even during hardship, God brings joy into our lives. "Weeping may tarry for the night, but joy comes with the morning" (v. 5). Praising God opens our hearts to joy, reminding us that no matter how dark the night feels or how long it lasts, God is at work, bringing light, life, and hope.

When you feel disconnected, unloved, lonely, numb, grieving, or filled with joy, praise brings you back to God. It's about letting God meet us right where we are. As we praise Him, we remember who He is and who we are in Him.

Write Your Own Praise Psalm

Writing a praise song is a soul-stirring way for you to connect with God for who He is, for what He has done in the past, and for what we know He will do in eternity. Forget perfection—let your words be raw and honest, expressing your gratitude for His endless love. Praising God lifts your spirit and draws you into His presence, turning even the simplest song into a moment of true worship.

1. Pour out your heart.

What do you want to share with God today? Write all of it down. Are you filled with gratitude? Awe? Maybe you need His comfort or want to celebrate His goodness. Whatever it is, don't hold anything back. God is here, ready to listen, eager to hear you. He cares deeply about every thought and feeling you have—so tell Him everything. You're safe with Him.

2. Get creative with imagery.

Have fun with your words! What images come to mind when you think of God's power and love? Maybe He's the solid rock when everything else feels shaky or His love is like a waterfall that never stops. Use vivid, creative language to paint a picture of who God is. Think big! God's glory is so incredible, and you get to capture that in your own unique way.

3. Be real.

How are you feeling, really? Be honest with God. If you're joyful, shout it out! If you're struggling, let Him know. Your Praise Psalm doesn't have to be flawless or polished. God loves the real you, even when your emotions are all over the place. Your story matters, and so does your journey. Bring your true self to the page and let your faith shine through, even if it's messy or a mix of highs and lows. God meets you right where you are.

4. Reflect on Jesus.

Think about how Jesus has changed everything. What does following Him mean to you? Remember, you have an incredible example to look up to—someone who knows your pain, who's walked in your shoes, and who's shown perfect love. How does that inspire your praise? You're part of a story full of hope and resurrection life. Let your psalm reflect that! Let your words overflow with the wonder of being loved and led by Jesus.

17. LOVED

28 Years

For Mike, I and love and you.

Psalm 100

1 Make a joyful noise to the LORD, all the earth!
2 Serve the LORD with gladness!
Come into His presence with singing!

3 Know that the LORD, He is God!
It is He who made us, and we are His;
we are His people, and the sheep of His pasture.

4 Enter His gates with thanksgiving,
and His courts with praise!
Give thanks to Him; bless His name!

5 For the LORD is good;
His steadfast love endures forever,
and His faithfulness to all generations.

Although I've been married most of my life, most days I feel like I'm still learning. Through days of routine and through exciting new seasons, I figure out a bit more all the time about what makes a lifelong relationship work.

Not only am I learning how to love Mike better, but I'm also learning how to be loved. Realizing that I'm fully known and fully loved is one of the most profound comforts in my life. But it's humbling to realize how much I need love. When my plans unravel or I'm consumed by doubt, the quiet assurance of being on the receiving end of this kind of love is a steadying presence. Since the beginning of our marriage, Mike's confidence in me encourages and enriches me when I question myself. His "I love you" is a drumbeat reminding me that I'm cherished. His leadership in our marriage and with our kids creates a safe environment.

Before I got married, the picture I had of what love looked like was drawn by my parents. They showed up for each other and for me in practical, sacrificial ways, teaching me about grace and responsibility. And the love I found in my marriage has added a whole new dimension to this picture.

Mike loves me with the kind of abundance I didn't know I didn't have. In the place our marriage has created, I found myself. It's like he has the exact nutrients my soul needs, and he gives them freely and in ways that make me believe they'll never run out. This love is the fire that warms me, the steady reassurance that gives me courage to dream.

Mike and I grow together, learn together, and evolve together as we navigate life. Because marriage isn't just about two people fitting together in a grand romance. It's a continuing adventure, discovering new ways to love when the old ones aren't enough. When the romantic love fades, when marriage feels monotonous, when challenges box us in, we look at each other and say, "We'll get through this. Together."

More than this though, marriage has deepened my understanding of God's love. Mike's strong faith in God shows me a tangible glimpse of the divine, the love that lasts. Every day, I'm in awe of the miracle that is marriage, this picture of God's love. This is the promise of Psalm 100: "For the Lord is good; His steadfast love endures forever, and His faithfulness to all generations" (v. 5).

Love, real love, isn't perfect. It's messy and hard. That's because we're sinful. We make mistakes, let others down, and put ourselves first. Even as I express how solid my marriage is, I know that all marriages are flawed and some marriages are harmful.

But a Christ-centered marriage is miraculous. That's because even when we're at our worst, we're forgiven, shown grace, and blessed through the people God puts in our lives.

And I'm endlessly grateful that God gave me you, Mike, to share it with.

ABOUT PSALM 100

"Praise God"

Psalm 100 overflows with the security that comes from being deeply loved. You know this feeling. It's safe. It's joy. It's a gift. And yet, God's love is even more powerful.

"From Whom All Blessings Flow"

In fact, Psalm 100 begins with a well-loved invitation to praise God: "Make a joyful noise to the LORD, all the earth!" (v. 1). This is a call for everything on earth to express joy for God and His love.

"Praise Him, All Creatures Here Below"

This love is based on God's everlasting grace, not on what you accomplished yesterday, how you act today, and what you will do tomorrow. "Know that the LORD, He is God! It is He who made us, and we are His; we are His people, and the sheep of His pasture" (v. 3).

"Praise Him Above, Ye Heavenly Host"

How do you respond to this powerful, secure, anchoring, constant love? Verse 4 encourages us to respond with praise: "Enter His gates with thanksgiving, and His courts with praise! Give thanks to Him; bless His name!" When we experience love, both human and divine, it stirs us to worship.

"Praise Father, Son, and Holy Ghost"

Through Christ, we see the ultimate act of love and grace. His sacrifice—His life, death, and resurrection—opened the door for us to be fully embraced by God. In Christ, we experience a love that is deeper and more secure than any love we've ever known.

Amen!

If you've ever felt totally loved by someone, Psalm 100 reminds you this is a faint picture of God's love for you. His love is steadfast forever.

DISCUSS PSALM 100

1. Who makes you feel loved?
2. Sing "Praise God, from Whom All Blessing Flow" (*LSB* 805) today, either by yourself or with a group.

PRAY

Lord, thank You for loving me with an everlasting love. When doubts and insecurities creep in, remind me of Your steadfast love that never fails. Help me to experience the joy of Your presence and to respond with a heart full of gratitude and praise. May Your love fill me with peace and assurance today and always. Amen.

18. LONELY

Don't Tell Me About Your Friends

For Connie, who has helped thousands feel less lonely, including me.

Psalm 27

1The LORD is my light and my salvation;
whom shall I fear?
The LORD is the stronghold of my life;
of whom shall I be afraid?

2When evildoers assail me
to eat up my flesh,
my adversaries and foes,
it is they who stumble and fall.

3Though an army encamp against me,
my heart shall not fear;
though war arise against me,
yet I will be confident.

4One thing have I asked of the LORD,
that will I seek after:
that I may dwell in the house of the LORD
all the days of my life,
to gaze upon the beauty of the LORD
and to inquire in His temple.

5For He will hide me in His shelter
in the day of trouble;

He will conceal me under the cover of His tent;
    He will lift me high upon a rock.

6 And now my head shall be lifted up
    above my enemies all around me,
and I will offer in His tent
    sacrifices with shouts of joy;
I will sing and make melody to the LORD.

7 Hear, O LORD, when I cry aloud;
    be gracious to me and answer me!
8 You have said, "Seek My face."
My heart says to You,
    "Your face, LORD, do I seek."
    9 Hide not Your face from me.
Turn not Your servant away in anger,
    O You who have been my help.
Cast me not off; forsake me not,
    O God of my salvation!
10 For my father and my mother have forsaken me,
    but the LORD will take me in.

11 Teach me Your way, O LORD,
    and lead me on a level path
    because of my enemies.
12 Give me not up to the will of my adversaries;
    for false witnesses have risen against me,
    and they breathe out violence.

13 I believe that I shall look upon the goodness of the LORD
    in the land of the living!
14 Wait for the LORD;
    be strong, and let your heart take courage;
    wait for the LORD!

How many friends are you supposed to have? That question is simple enough, right? But no one seems to know. Some people say you need only a few close friends, enough to count on just one hand. Others insist you need a full party bus of friends—different people for every part of life. And then there's the idea that you should have at least one friend for each mood: someone for serious talks, someone for silly adventures, someone to understand you when you're down. But who's keeping score? How do we actually find out how many friends we should have? And why does the friend count matter?

In a world where we're connected all the time, loneliness still finds a way to creep in. This feeling doesn't just happen when we're alone, though. It feels like no one quite gets us, like we're invisible even in a crowd. Loneliness whispers, "You're missing something." "If you had just one more friend, you'd be whole." "No one is with you in this." Loneliness isn't fixed by numbers. It isn't resolved when we have more confidants in our inner circle. Loneliness is about feeling known and understood and accepted. When those things are missing, the ache can be tough to shake.

It's tempting to try to drown out that ache by staying busy, scrolling, or adding people to fill the silence. Any of those things is easier than facing loneliness head-on. But here's the thing—these psalms show us a different way to handle loneliness. Instead of covering it up or ignoring it, they invite us to bring it out into the open and talk to God about it. Page after page, these psalms give us a real path to turn loneliness into connection with Him.

To be honest with you, loneliness has often been a part of my story. For example, I switched schools in seventh grade, going from a tiny private school where I knew literally everyone to a huge public school where I didn't know a soul. Walking those unfamiliar, endless hallways without a friend to look to, feeling like an outsider—that's the kind of loneliness that sticks with you.

Sometimes loneliness returns when I travel and I see people who are setting off on adventures, their energy level high and eyes wide with excitement. Or it returns when I spend too much time working alone and a fog of sadness settles over me. The too familiar ache of being left out, of being on the outside looking in, returns.

In those moments, loneliness spins its lies: "You'll always feel this way." "Something's wrong with you." But I've learned to see those lies for what they are: the temptation to focus on myself, to make myself the main character of my story. But truth is that ache doesn't mean I'm unlovable; it means I'm wired to connect—with others and with Him. So I give those thoughts and feelings to God.

Loneliness loves to convince us we're the only ones who feel this way. But God's truth tells a different story. David lays it all out for God: "Turn to me and be gracious to me, for I am lonely and afflicted" (Psalm 25:16). In David's words, we see that loneliness isn't a dead end. It's a path that can lead us closer to God.

When we bring our loneliness to Him, it opens a door. We don't have to cover it up. We can let Him see us fully, confess our weakness, and ask for His mercy. In that intimacy, God fills us with His love. When we pray those same words from these psalms, we're not alone. We're part of a big, beautiful group of people across generations who've lifted these same prayers to the Lord—people who've cried out in moments of isolation, heartbreak, or grief. Together, we've looked for refuge and found it in God, knowing that, with Him, we are connected in a way that loneliness can't shake.

So, if you feel that ache, let it lead you back to God. Like David, open up to your heavenly Father. Tell Him your worries, your questions, your desire to be seen. You're not praying alone. You're part of an unending chorus of voices all seeking love and comfort in Him. And you're held by the God who created you and knows every corner of your heart. Our compassionate God never leaves you to face loneliness alone. Let that truth wrap around you, now and always.

ABOUT PSALM 27

Psalm 27 is such a comforting reminder that, even in our loneliest moments, God is right here with us. David starts with such a bold statement: "The LORD is my light and my salvation; whom shall I fear? The LORD is the stronghold of my life; of whom shall I be afraid?" (v. 1).

Loneliness can make us feel vulnerable, like we're all by ourselves in the world, but this psalm speaks right to that. God is our light, guiding us through the darkest times, and He's the stronghold that holds us steady when we feel like we're slipping.

Light & Salvation

Psalm 27 gives us a real sense that Jesus is the steady, unshakable presence in our life. When David says, "The LORD is my light and my salvation; whom shall I fear? The LORD is the stronghold of my life; of whom shall I be afraid?" (v. 1), it points to the heart of Christ's role in our lives. Psalm 27 is a picture of Jesus standing by us, reminding us that, with Him, we're never alone, and there's nothing we need to fear.

Remember, in your loneliest moments, you are not truly alone. Christ is your light, your stronghold, and your safe place.

Yet, I Will Be Confident

David responds to his feelings of fear and isolation with trust. "Though an army encamp against me, my heart shall not fear; though war arise against me, yet I will be confident" (v. 3). Even when he's facing overwhelming situations, David knows that God is present with him and that is enough. No matter how alone we feel, God's love never changes, and that gives us confidence to keep going, even when we're struggling.

Dwell in the House of the Lord

One of the most beautiful parts of Psalm 27 is David's desire to simply be close to God: "One thing have I asked of the LORD, that will I seek after: that I may dwell in the house of the LORD all the days of my life" (v. 4).

David longs to be near God, to dwell in His presence because that's where true connection and peace are found. Loneliness identifies for us that we crave deeper connection, and this psalm gently reminds us that God is the ultimate answer to that longing. His presence fills the spaces where we feel most alone, offering us a love that never leaves.

Never, Ever Abandoned

David also acknowledges the pain of feeling abandoned: "For my father and my mother have forsaken me, but the LORD will take me in" (v. 10). When even the people closest to us let us down or when relationships fall apart, God's love remains constant. He promises to never leave us behind, and His arms are always open to bring us close. It is such a beautiful reassurance that God never fails us. His love is steady, reliable, and always there to hold us and protect us.

DISCUSS PSALM 27

1. Do the frantic pace of modern life and demands of social media leave you feeling lonely? Write about that here.

2. Read Psalm 27 again. Which promises remind you of God's everlasting love?

PRAY

Dear Jesus, my loneliness weighs heavy on my heart. Remind me of Your promise that You never leave me nor forsake me. Draw me close to You, my light and salvation, and fill me with Your peace and presence. Help me to find comfort in knowing that You are with me always, guiding me with Your love. Amen.

19. NUMB

Screaming Toddlers, Yelling Teenagers & Crying Christians

For Aunt Katie, who prays for screaming toddlers, yelling teens, and crying Christians.

Psalm 13

1 How long, Lord? Will You forget me forever?
How long will You hide your face from me?
2 How long must I take counsel in my soul
and have sorrow in my heart all the day?
How long shall my enemy be exalted over me?

3 Consider and answer me, O Lord my God;
light up my eyes, lest I sleep the sleep of death,
4 lest my enemy say, "I have prevailed over him,"
lest my foes rejoice because I am shaken.

5 But I have trusted in Your steadfast love;
my heart shall rejoice in Your salvation.
6 I will sing to the Lord,
because He has dealt bountifully with me.

Right now, all four of my kids are teenagers. The youngest is thirteen, the oldest is nineteen, and the twins in the middle are sixteen. We haven't had this much emotion in our house since the years when our youngest was two, our oldest was eight, and our twins were loud, chaotic kids in the middle.

As a coach for teenagers, I help my clients talk about their feelings. Together, we figure out why they struggle to express fear, anger, or sadness, and we work through those emotions to help them reach their goals. All this to say, I'm super comfortable with a lot of raw emotion.

Which is why the complaints at the beginning of Psalm 13 are like the soundtrack to my life right now. David's lament about how his life isn't going well? I hear you, David. He's full of angst, impatience, and frustration, which is pretty much the human experience for teenagers and toddlers.

When our kids were between the ages of 1 and 6, tantrums were loud, unstoppable expressions of all their angst. Sure, they often didn't understand exactly why they were crying or screaming, but they felt safe enough to let it all out. "I ONLY DRINK FROM THE RED CUP." "THE TOOTHPASTE IS TOO SPICY." "I NEED MY CHICKEN NUGGETS." Whether or not the emotions made sense, they poured out all over the place.

Teenagers aren't much different. Most of them are also good at letting you know how they feel. They'll rant about the injustices they see, complain about needing more freedom or money, or vent about feeling overwhelmed. In my house and in my coaching sessions, teens laugh, cry, fight, and passionately express every emotion and opinion. And that's healthy.

What worries me more are the adolescents who stay silent, hiding behind endless scrolling or isolating themselves behind closed doors. Everyone who has cared for a toddler knows that noise usually means everything is fine. The real concern comes when things are quiet—when you turn the corner and find the dog covered in your best face wash.

Teenagers are similar: Their complaints and emotional outbursts are often signs that things are okay. It's when they become withdrawn that our radar goes up. Those glassy stares, monosyllabic answers, and long hours of isolation can be signs they're struggling.

This brings us back to David in Psalm 13. When he cries out to God in verses 1–4, it's not a quiet, composed prayer. He's brutally honest, venting his frustration that God hasn't fixed things that he knows God is powerful enough to resolve. David feels safe enough to lament, to complain about being abandoned and disappointed. And that's important because that kind of faith is more real than a hundred "Let go and let God" memes. Deep down, David knows God can handle his anger, his disappointment, his mess.

This reminder to honestly feel our emotions and express them to God is crucial. Telling God we're unhappy with our circumstances is an act of authentic faith, not weakness. It acknowledges that God's love for us isn't dependent on our pretending everything is okay and saying the "right" things. God is omniscient. He sees our genuine grief and hurt—and He still loves us.

But Psalm 13 doesn't end there. Once he has confessed these feelings, once he has gotten this off his chest, David remembers that God is a God of unfailing love. Despite all the pain and doubt, he holds on to that truth. And as modern Christians, we have an even clearer picture of God's goodness because it's wrapped up in Jesus—His birth in Bethlehem, His crown of thorns, His resurrection. David didn't know those details, but he trusted that God's goodness would come through, that His love would endure because God promised that it would.

So, bring your complaints to God. Tell Him where you're struggling. Cry, ask questions, and cast blame. God can take it. He is powerful, all knowing, and right there with you. Most of all, He loves you. He gave you Jesus, and that divine, unconditional love is the ultimate ending to every story of struggle.

Take a moment to reflect on the hurts you're carrying. Imagine them as piercing arrows life has shot at you: being left out, feeling disappointed by your family, carrying the burden of grief for loved ones gone too soon, or experiencing the paralysis of not knowing what's next. Let yourself feel the pain of those arrows. They hurt. You are not invincible.

Now, like David, ask God to remind you of His love. Ask Him to help you see His goodness even in the darkness. As you sit with both the grief and the good, take a deep breath. Remember that God is with you, hearing you, sharing your pain, and loving you. Forever.

ABOUT PSALM 13

When you feel emotionally worn out, numbness settles in. David's words remind you that you don't have to pretend everything's fine. You can be real with God, even when you're struggling to feel anything at all.

Trust in His Love

After pouring out his pain, David says, "But I have trusted in Your steadfast love; my heart shall rejoice in Your salvation" (v. 5). His circumstances haven't changed, but his focus has. David chooses to trust in God's love, even when everything else feels off.

This is an important reminder. God's love doesn't depend on feelings. His love is constant, even when we're numb to it.

He's Been So Good to Me

David's final words, "I will sing to the LORD, because He has dealt bountifully with me" (v. 6), are thanksgiving for His blessings. He chooses to worship, not because he feels like it but because he remembers God's goodness.

Worship becomes a way to reconnect with God's constant love, even when we don't feel it. Choosing to praise or pray when we're emotionally exhausted can break through the numbness. That's because the Holy Spirit is working in us, constantly strengthening our faith.

Jesus as the Bridge

In David's cry, we hear echoes of Jesus' own experience. On the cross, Jesus felt the full weight of human suffering that included the physical pain of torture and the pain of knowing He was separated from God. By His sacrifice, Jesus made sure that we will never be separated from God, no matter how distant we feel. We will never know the pain of not having God with us. Our Savior's love bridges the gap between our numbness and God's presence.

DISCUSS PSALM 13

1. If you've been through a season of spiritual numbness, what caused it? Describe how it felt to be paralyzed by grief, pain, fear, or shame.

2. When you feel numb, what comfort do you find in the Lord? His love? His patience with you? His Word and Sacrament? The reminder of the blessings He has given you? Write about those here.

PRAY

Lord God, You see all my feelings, every disappointment, what I'm grieving, and why I'm heartbroken about the pain of this life. You know my sorrow, my impatience, and the hurt I carry with me. Thank You, Lord, for hearing all this. You love me so much that I know I can experience all this and Your love never fails. I will praise You forever because of that love. Keep pulling me out of my numbness so I can know Your healing and perfect care. In Jesus' name. Amen.

20. GRIEVING

The Generations Get Shorter

For Lydia, we miss you so much. For Lanie, who misses you the most.

Psalm 121

1 I lift up my eyes to the hills.
From where does my help come?
2 My help comes from the LORD,
who made heaven and earth.

3 He will not let your foot be moved;
He who keeps you will not slumber.
4 Behold, He who keeps Israel
will neither slumber nor sleep.

5 The LORD is your keeper;
the LORD is your shade on your right hand.
6 the sun will not strike you by day,
nor the moon by night.

7 The LORD will keep you from all evil;
He will keep your life.
8 the LORD will keep
your going out and your coming in
from this time forth and forevermore.

Every year, as graduation season rolls around, I feel a familiar ache. Watching each new group of kids cross that stage, stepping into the next chapter, always makes me aware that time is spinning forward.

It's happy, of course—this celebration of growth, dreams, and possibilities. But beneath the excitement, I feel a deep sadness in watching them go. These kids, who came in as freshmen and became part of the fabric of our school, are leaving. And as each student moves on, they take a little piece of the world as I know it. This season always brings up the same questions: How do we say goodbye? How do we keep going in a world that changes so quickly, in ways that feel so permanent? I wonder how to grieve what time takes from us.

Grief—change, really—asks us to leave behind what has shaped us. And this is a complex feeling. We experience both the joy of growth and the sadness of letting go. Our loved ones leave, kids go to college, eras pass, people pass, and experiences end. These changes are fragments in a much larger story that is constantly being written. What is difficult is that these memories comprise our understanding, our knowledge of our lives, and at the same time they tell us that we can't go back but can only go forward into the next day—into the unknown future without these times and without these people as they are right now.

Life is a series of leave-takings. People move, families shift, seasons change, jobs start and stop. It's easy to feel that we're the only ones witnessing these moments, the only ones seeing each small farewell, each last look. And in one sense, that's true. Only we know what each goodbye means to us. But in another, we're never alone. Psalm 121 paints a picture of God as our keeper, intimately involved in each "coming and going" with a steady, unfailing presence. Our sovereign God knows every detail of our past and every aspect of our future. And He holds all of it with a love and a power that never wavers.

Grief in these moments comes from moving forward without those familiar places and people. It's the weight of everything you have known pressed into each step toward the unknown. There's an ache in this grief that God knows very well. He's been there, in every place you've left, in every face you've loved. But He is already in the places you are heading. He is fully present, walking with you, leading you, carrying you, protecting you, and waiting for you to arrive. God is not a distant witness; He travels every inch of this journey with you.

The comforting knowledge that we belong to God and that He holds each moment in His hands as part of His plan for those who love Him is the solid ground we travel. His intimate involvement is the foundation under each step, the assurance that we're wrapped in something stronger than our own ability to remember. Nothing slips past His notice. He's seen it all—the big events, the minutia, and everything in between; the moments we keep replaying; the memories we hold close; and the places we'll need to release. He knows what we'll miss, what we hold dear, and exactly what waits on the other side.

We belong to God. He holds every moment—every step, every breath—in His hands. His care is steady, like the ground beneath our feet and as constant as the sky overhead.

Nothing escapes His attention. Nothing is lost.

Jesus walks with us in it all. He knows the weight we carry—the memories we cherish, the ones that ache, the ones we're unsure how to hold. He sees our hearts stretched between what was and what's still to come. He understands the longing, the joy, the waiting.

God knows what we will miss, what we will cling to, and what we will need to release. He sees what's ahead—the goodness just beyond our sight. Through every shift and season, Jesus remains near. We are known, kept, and loved. And that is enough.

ABOUT PSALM 121

From Where Does My Help Come?

Psalm 121 is one of those psalms that feels like drawing a deep breath when you're grieving. It starts with a simple but powerful question: "I lift up my eyes to the hills. From where does my help come?" (v. 1).

When we're in the middle of grief, it can feel like we're searching for something, anything, to help us keep going. The psalmist quickly answers this question: "My help comes from the LORD, who made heaven and earth" (v. 2). Right from the start, we're reminded that in our deepest sorrow, God holds us together. The one who made everything has our lives under control. He cares intimately about what we're going through.

God Does Not Slumber

Grief can be such a lonely experience. It can feel like no one can fully understand the depth of our pain. But Psalm 121 offers this incredibly comforting truth: "He will not let your foot be moved; He who keeps you will not slumber" (v. 3). When we feel like the weight of grief might knock us off balance, God is there, keeping us steady, holding us close, helping us put one foot in front of the other.

Protecting Your Heart, Mind & Soul

David says, "The LORD will keep you from all evil; He will keep your life" (v. 7). Grief often makes us feel like everything is falling apart, and it's hard to believe that we can be kept safe in that storm. But this verse reminds us that our Lord protects our hearts, our minds, our souls. Think about the account of Jesus in the boat with His disciples. Our heavenly Father's presence is that shelter in the middle of a storm. The storm might still rage, but He is there to keep us safe with Him. Yes, it might feel like everything around us is out of control, but is it really? The one who keeps the sun rising and the earth spinning also holds us in His hand, protects us from evil, and promises us healing and peace with Him in eternity.

Both Now & Forevermore

One of the most comforting promises in Psalm 121 is at the very end: "The LORD will keep your going out and your coming in from this time forth and forevermore" (v. 8). When we're grieving, the future can feel so uncertain, and we don't know how to move forward or what to do about what comes next. But this verse reassures us that God is with us not just in this painful moment but in all the days ahead. He's walking with us now, caring about us when we're stumbling through our grief, and healing us by His Spirit. We can let go of our worry about what's coming next because it is in His control. God is already there, watching over us with love.

DISCUSS PSALM 121

1. What grief are you carrying with you? How does it feel? What parts of life have disappointed you? What parts have left you in pain?
2. Look at Psalm 121 again. What aspects of God's character comfort you?

PRAY

Father, Creator and Sustainer of everything, comfort me when I am grieving. Remind me that even as life changes, Your love endures. Thank You for watching over me and being my ever-present help in times of trouble. Lift my spirit and renew my hope as I lean on Your promises. May Your presence bring peace and healing to my heart. Amen.

21. JOY

Run Your Race, Girl

For Renee, I can't believe we did this.

Psalm 30

1 I will extol You, O LORD, for You have drawn me up
and have not let my foes rejoice over me.
2 O LORD my God, I cried to You for help,
and You have healed me.
3 O LORD, You have brought up my soul from Sheol;
You restored me to life from among those who go down to the pit.

4 Sing praises to the LORD, O you His saints,
and give thanks to His holy name.
5 For His anger is but for a moment,
and His favor is for a lifetime.
Weeping may tarry for the night,
but joy comes with the morning.

6 As for me, I said in my prosperity,
"I shall never be moved."
7 By Your favor, O LORD,
You made my mountain stand strong;
You hid Your face;
I was dismayed.

8 To You, O LORD, I cry,
and to the LORD I plead for mercy:

9 "What profit is there in my death,
 if I go down to the pit?
Will the dust praise You?
 Will it tell of Your faithfulness?
10 Hear, O LORD, and be merciful to me!
 O LORD, be my helper!"

11 You have turned for me my mourning into dancing;
 You have loosed my sackcloth
 and clothed me with gladness,
12 that my glory may sing Your praise and not be silent.
 O LORD my God, I will give thanks to You forever!

We are a running family. It started with Mike. He's a low-key, logical guy, who thrives on routine. He also regularly races twenty-six miles. Each marathon is different, so his running them seems like a juxtaposition to his daily life, yet he loves it and is good at it. There's something captivating about watching that passion.

When our kids were little, we went to all his races. We were his cheering section in matching T-shirts, clutching race maps, waving encouraging signs, and going on movie-worthy chase scenes to find him along the course and glimpse him running.

We love seeing the crowd of runners pounding toward us with Mike right in the middle. His head is down, he's tired, and we're yelling his name. He looks up, grins at all of us screaming fools, and runs harder.

I cry every time we see him during every marathon. Not just because of the adrenaline-fueled frenzy of calculating his pace and following his course amid thousands of runners. I cry because of the enormous effort of all the athletes—the wrinkly, saggy men in their eighth decade, the hyper-fit runners who glisten with sweat from their freakishly fast pace, and the middle-aged parents who were too busy to train properly. They all give everything they have on race morning.

Through all those years that Mike was passionate about running and I was passionate about cheering for him, our children were paying attention. They loved every morning that I woke them before dawn to sit in a cold car to track their dad's race. They absorbed all the talk about split times and pace and PRs. And the four of them decided that running is where it's at.

So, while other girls learned to spike volleyballs, our girls learned to properly lace track spikes. While other boys were mastering layups, our boys were laying down miles.

They are physically built for running and quickly discovered that most kids didn't love circling the track in triple-digit Texas heat. Our three older kids each won a triathlon before they were out of elementary school. Sam ran a marathon when he was fourteen. Elisabeth set records in middle school. When Catie wanted a social media account, we told her she had to run fifty miles to show us she was serious about it. And she did.

Through it all, I watched and screamed and cheered. I grew up in a blue-collar town in the eighties where no one was invested in girls' sports. Girl runner? I didn't know any. I could video my family's races but couldn't run one myself. I could talk about prerace jitters and carb-loading but had never experienced it first hand.

Then, I started to wonder, could I run a big race? After two decades of being so invested in my family's races, what about me?

One day, my friend Renee said she was running the Houston Half Marathon for her fiftieth birthday. She has been an athlete all her life. She works as a physical therapist. She is also super down to earth. If I were to pick a role model to start a midlife running practice, Renee would be it. Without thinking, I said I would do it too.

Announcing in front of a dozen of our friends that I would run a half marathon felt great—until I realized that now I had to do it.

Regret and hard work followed.

The training was terrible. I lacked some fundamental grit. I ran each mile with ridiculous bursts of rationale: "I will pretend a dragon is chasing me to the stop sign." "I will run until the end of this song; actually, until the end of the chorus." "If I run four miles on Monday, I don't have to even look at my running shoes until Thursday."

The kids were honestly confused by my hatred for running. "You're being dramatic," the girls told me. "You're pretty slow," the boys confirmed. Mike, who had invited me on hundreds of runs, was ecstatic that I was out there trying.

In the weeks before race day, I started to panic. Renee was (literally) miles ahead of me. She had pacing strategies, a stretching routine, a finish-time goal, and energy gels, goos, and gummies. She had also run the required thirteen miles lots of times. A week before the race, my farthest run was seven miles. Even Mike, my most excited cheerleader, was getting worried.

Race day came and the weather was perfect. Renee and I showed up ridiculously early and went to the church service, hoping to calm our nerves. My pockets were filled with gel packets and my muscles were as ready as they would be.

Renee was nursing an injury and said I would be faster. This was laughable. I couldn't imagine being faster than any of the other anxious runners who pressed against me as we corralled at the start line.

Renee and I took a selfie before we started and there is real terror in my eyes—the look of a soldier before a doomed war, a little kid walking into a dark forest, a geeky teen looking for a table in the middle school cafeteria.

Then, I started to run—so, so slowly and with a rushing tide of runners passing me on either side. I was making progress though. By the one-mile marker (already one mile!), Renee said to go ahead so she could pace herself a little slower. And even though my legs were not very strong, my excitement was.

Here's what I hadn't planned on: the crowds! They were thick along the sides of the road, and they were so excited. Funny signs, speakers pumping out eighties rap, people shouting "You got this!" It electrified me. I could feel their enthusiasm.

I started to cry and did not stop for the next twelve miles.

Even as I type this, I'm blinking away tears. All those Houstonians, all that exuberance, all the pure human effort—I could not get enough of it. Maybe it was the energy gels I was sucking down, but my body was pounding with vitality.

And then, I rounded a corner and my family was there screaming.

Oh my, y'all. To see my kids and Mike, all of them there with their shirts and signs. It just undid me. My knees weakened, and I could have stopped right there to soak in the joy of that moment.

But I didn't because they were shouting for me to "Go! Run faster!" and all the other ridiculous things we yell during races. I wiped my wet face and just kept going.

I never slowed down. It was too good. I finished with a very slow time, of course. Many runners finished the full marathon in the time it took me to run half, but I did not care at all. I found Renee as we finished, and we hugged and cried.

The joy pounded through me for all of it. Yes, my legs were sore. My brain was fizzy from all the emotion and adrenaline. My stomach rebelled against all that gooey energy.

But my heart was just bursting with happiness.

This is joy.

This is what it feels like when we see how God has been taking care of us the whole time. This is recognizing that even when we are scared or distracted or angry, God is still all powerful, all loving, and all knowing—all for us.

This is the delight we have as His people. This is the ecstasy we celebrate on Christmas, when we thank God for the gift of His Son, and the bliss we celebrate on Easter, when we thank Him for our eternal life.

This is the joy we celebrate every single moment as children of our Lord, whose love endures forever.

ABOUT PSALM 30

This is such a beautiful reminder that real joy often comes after we've walked through a hard time. Already in the first verse, we hear David's relief: "I will extol You, O LORD, for You have drawn me up and have not let my foes rejoice over me" (v. 1). You can feel the weight lifting from David's heart. You can feel the building joy.

Feel it now. Feel the joy in your life. Feel that sunshine in your brain when you see the blessings God gives you.

Morning Joy and Dancing

Thousands of years later, David's description of joy still resonates. One of the most encouraging parts is verse 5: "Weeping may tarry for the night, but joy comes with the morning." This. For all of us who have cried through the long, dark night, joy comes with the light.

God is the one who turns our sorrow into dancing: "You have turned for me my mourning into dancing; You have loosed my sackcloth and clothed me with gladness" (v. 11). Our Father takes away the sackcloth, a rough mourning garment, and replaces it with this beautiful, energetic expression of life. God transforms our sorrow. Joy is possible. From condemnation to Gospel, from pain to relief, from dark to light, from mourning to dancing.

Joy Rooted in Trust

That God's timing is perfect is perhaps the hardest part of trust. "O LORD my God, I cried to You for help, and You have healed me" (v. 2). When the healing—the joy—takes longer than we want, it's so easy to give up. There are nights that feel long and mornings that feel far away. But this psalm assures us that God hears us. The joy that comes is richer because we've experienced God's faithfulness along the way.

The Ultimate Joy

Jesus turned the sorrow of our sin into our joy. David praises God for restoring his life (v. 3), and this is what Jesus does for us. His resurrection on Easter was the "morning after the night" moment.

Joy broke through the sorrow, defeated sin, and rose victorious over death. This is why we sing for joy—because Jesus lives and reigns now, filling every moment with His presence and the promise of eternal life.

Psalm 30 teaches us that God brings us through the darkness of earthly life to something better. We might weep, but joy is coming, and when it does, it will be like the sun breaking through after a storm.

DISCUSS PSALM 30

1. What words in Psalm 30 inspire you to see joy in God's presence, even when life feels dark?
2. Share your favorite words from the psalm. What specific phrases resonate with you?

PRAY

Heavenly Father, thank You for the joy that comes from knowing You and experiencing Your goodness in my life now and from knowing the joy that comes in eternity. When I am in darkness, remind me of Your faithfulness and Your blessings that surround me. Help me to rejoice always, knowing that You are my source of true happiness. May my heart overflow with gratitude and praise for Your unfailing, everlasting love. In Jesus' name. Amen.

Messianic Psalms

The stone that the builders rejected has become the cornerstone. Psalm 118:22

The Messianic Psalms remind us that, even in our hardest moments, God's love for us has always been in motion. Long before we were ever aware of it, God was working out His plan of salvation through His Son, Jesus. These psalms give us hope, showing that God's promises have been fulfilled in Christ, even when life feels uncertain, overwhelming, or impossible. When we feel crushed by life, unsure of where to turn, or filled with gratitude for all that God has done, the Messianic Psalms help us remember that God is always at work, drawing us back to Himself.

The Lord of Hosts (Psalm 46)

God is our refuge and strength, and we are never alone. Psalm 46 reminds us we're connected to something bigger. In moments when we long to feel connected and secure, we can remember that Jesus, our constant source of belonging, is with us: "The LORD of hosts is with us; the God of Jacob is our fortress" (v. 7).

Faithfulness to All Generations (Psalm 89)

When you feel crushed, read Psalm 89. "How long, O LORD? Will You hide Yourself forever? How long will Your wrath burn like fire?" (v. 46). This is the heartache of wondering where God is in our suffering. But even in the heaviness, the psalmist clings to hope: "I will sing of the steadfast love of the LORD, forever; with my mouth I will make known Your faithfulness to all generations" (v. 1).

Jesus was crushed when He bore the weight of our sin on the cross. But through His suffering, God's love and faithfulness shone brighter than ever. When we feel crushed, we can hold on to the truth that Jesus has already walked through the deepest pain for us. God's steadfast love hasn't left us—He walks with us through every difficult moment.

Our Stronghold (Psalm 94)

Feeling unsure about what to do next? Psalm 94 acknowledges our deep desire for God to give the next steps in His plan. As a Messianic Psalm, it reminds us that God's timing is perfect, even when we can't see it. It's a call to trust in God's plan that Jesus, the promised Redeemer, will bring true justice. Place your hope in God. Believe He is actively working, even when the path feels unclear.

Our Joyful Noise (Psalm 95)

Psalm 95 is for the seasons when your heart overflows with gratitude. "Oh come, let us sing to the LORD; let us make a joyful noise to the rock of our salvation!" (v. 1). Celebrate God's goodness and recognize that every good thing is from Him. "For the LORD is a great God, and a great King above all gods" (v. 3). Let this psalm remind you that Christ's goodness is unchanging and His love is forever.

My favorite message of the Messianic Psalms is the vivid examples of God's grace. It's not our strength but Jesus' sacrifice that brings us into a relationship with God. The Messianic Psalms reflect this beautifully. They point us to Jesus—the one who carries our burdens, the one who gave us new life through His death and resurrection. These psalms are a reminder that God's plan for us has always been one of redemption and, through Christ, we are made new.

Write Your Own Messianic Psalm

Writing your own Messianic Psalm gives you the chance to dive into something truly extraordinary. These psalms are full of prophetic glimpses of the Savior and paint vivid pictures of who Jesus is, what He does, and the hope He brings. As you explore these ancient songs, let your heart be moved by the way they point to Christ and show you God's incredible plan to redeem and restore.

1. Start with the heaviness.

What feels impossible to carry alone? Maybe it's the crushing weight of anxiety or the ache of dreams that never came true. Messianic Psalms invite you to name this weight and bring it to God, the one who's strong enough to carry you through the storm.

2. Describe the darkness.

How does this struggle look in your mind? Let your words bring these images to life. Psalms are prayers, and they don't always have pretty language. Instead, paint a picture of your reality. God meets you there, right in the mess of it.

3. Ask the deep questions.

What haunts you in the quiet moments? Do you wonder if God sees your pain or why He hasn't shown up yet? Ask all of that. Messianic Psalms give you space to lay those pieces out before God.

4. Recall the promises.

What truths have carried you before? Remember His faithfulness. Think of what you've witnessed and write about that. Messianic Psalms hold on to these glimpses of light, even when they're faint. Trust that what God has promised still stands.

5. Hold on to hope.

How does hope feel right now? Maybe it's fragile. Write it anyway. Trust that even when you can't see it, God is moving, working, redeeming. Messianic Psalms remind us that Jesus is coming again and, with Him, a new world is waiting. Write about that truth specifically.

22. SECURE

Yelling. Pounding. Fire. Ritual.

For Will, may your heart stay secure in the Lord.
Proverbs 24:17. Zap. Boom.

Psalm 46

1God is our refuge and strength,
a very present help in trouble.
2Therefore we will not fear though the earth gives way,
though the mountains be moved into the heart of the sea,
3though its waters roar and foam,
though the mountains tremble at its swelling. *Selah*

4There is a river whose streams make glad the city of God,
the holy habitation of the Most High.
5God is in the midst of her; she shall not be moved;
God will help her when morning dawns.
6The nations rage, the kingdoms totter;
He utters His voice, the earth melts.
7The Lord of hosts is with us;
the God of Jacob is our fortress. *Selah*

8Come, behold the works of the Lord,
how He has brought desolations on the earth.
9He makes wars cease to the end of the earth;
He breaks the bow and shatters the spear;
He burns the chariots with fire.

[10]"Be still, and know that I am God.
I will be exalted among the nations,
I will be exalted in the earth!"
[11]The LORD of hosts is with us;
the God of Jacob is our fortress. *Selah*

For many decades, our family has been part of Camp Lone Star. This place is so significant to us that every summer when I return, it feels like I'm stepping on holy ground. Which, I suppose, I am. After all, for more than eighty years, this ministry has shared the love of Jesus with hundreds of thousands of guests.

Some of my earliest memories took place in these musty cabins. Ditto for my kids, who have spent countless hours canoeing and hiking over the fifty acres. They belong here as much as I do.

At Camp Lone Star, one of the biggest events of the summer is Race for the Kingdom, RFTK for short. It's an epic, campwide showdown that is packed with fierce competition and team loyalty. It has been a tradition for as long as anyone can remember. For Camp Lone Star enthusiasts, RFTK isn't just a game—it's a defining experience, the moment you find your people. Being a Blue Bolt or a Gray Gladiator is a part of who you are for the summer, maybe even for life.

The Split kicks it all off. Campers step up, one by one, to find out which side they'll fight for. It might look over the top to an outsider, maybe even a little strange. It's more than just a sorting ceremony since, in that single moment, each camper discovers where they fit. There's something electric in it.

Last summer at the Split, I watched as a family friend walked up to the big wooden star in the center of the pavilion. The clearing was lined with metal barrels with fire inside, flames shooting up into the night sky. On one side, the Gladiators chanted and pounded their fists. On the other, the Bolts were screaming just as loudly.

Our friend looked around, a little unsure and maybe feeling the weight of what was about to happen. The spotlight swept across the sky, searching, until it stopped on him. For a second, everything stilled. Then, the light shifted to his side—the Blue Bolts.

The Bolts erupted. They cheered his name, high-fived him, and pulled him right in. Just like that, he belonged. He wasn't a mere camper anymore; he was one of them.

Watching it, I thought about how powerful this moment really is. It isn't just about a camp rivalry. It's about belonging, finding your people, and knowing you're part of something.

As he joined his camp family, I was reminded of Psalm 46, which speaks of an even greater truth: No matter where we go, we belong to God. He's our fortress, our place of strength and safety. Belonging to Him is the ultimate comfort. And just as our friend was welcomed by his team, by Baptism we are welcomed into a greater family—our Christian family—who cheers us on and lifts us up when we're weak. Yes, God is always there, strong and steady, like a fortress. He also surrounds us with people who remind us of His love and give us courage when we need it.

There's something beautiful in both kinds of belonging, in finding your people here on earth and in knowing you're eternally in the family of God. And at Camp Lone Star, with all the chants and flames and friendships, we catch a glimpse of the deeper truth that while we may feel pulled in many directions, our true belonging is secure. We belong to God, who is our refuge and strength, a fortress we can always trust.

ABOUT PSALM 46

"A Mighty Fortress Is Our God"

Psalm 46 talks about God's rock-solid presence and protection. It reminds you that you belong to a community rooted in God's strength. For generations, this psalm has offered comfort and inspiration. This is the deep bond we share as we find our refuge in the

Lord together. Martin Luther wrote the beloved hymn "A Mighty Fortress Is Our God" about this exactly.

"A Trusty Shied and Weapon"

This psalm was written when Israel faced war and destruction. The vivid imagery of natural disasters and warfare expresses the dangers that God's people encountered. What about us as modern believers? What attacks do we face? How does the church bond together to support one another?

"He Holds the Field Forever"

The sons of Korah, who wrote this psalm, were the worship leaders in the temple. They led the people in worship as a powerful, shared experience. Picture being part of that, lifting your voice with a crowd of people who all trust God together. In Psalm 46, we see the strength of a shared community. Belonging to something bigger—a family grounded in faith—is part of our shared hope.

Can you feel that hope now? Think about where you belong. Know the security it provides and the hope to be included in a group of believers.

"We Tremble Not, We Fear No Ill"

Psalm 46 opens with a powerful statement: "God is our refuge and strength, a very present help in trouble" (v. 1). This verse sets the tone for the entire prayer, as it celebrates that God is a haven for His people. Even if the world collapses—mountains falling into the sea or waters roaring with fury—God is our fortress, our ever-present source of strength.

In verses 4–5, we have the image of a river whose streams bring joy to the "city of God." God's peace flows through the community of believers, even when we're surrounded by threats. We trust that nothing is stronger than the love of Christ and the power of the Holy Spirit.

"For Us Fights the Valiant One"

Twice, Psalm 46 declares, "The LORD of hosts is with us; the God of Jacob is our fortress" (vv. 7, 11). This is a reminder that we are God's people. This is belonging.

"The LORD of hosts" points to God as the commander of heavenly armies, a powerful protector who fights for His people. The repetition of "with us" reassures us that God's presence unites His people in faith and hope. This belonging provides solidarity even during life's fiercest battles.

"On Earth Is Not His Equal"

Jesus, who fulfills the promise of God's everlasting presence, is the point of Psalm 46. Through His life, death, and resurrection, He secured our eternal safety, offering us a place in God's unshakable kingdom. When we face turmoil, we remember Jesus' words: "In the world you will have tribulation. But take heart; I have overcome the world" (John 16:33).

This psalm is a powerful reminder that our true belonging is found in Christ. As members of His Body, we are united in His victory, standing firm together with God as our refuge and strength.

Hymn lyrics are from *LSB* 656.

DISCUSS PSALM 46

1. How does Psalm 46 help you find security in God's presence rather than in worldly circumstances?

2. What practices can help you draw closer to God and strengthen your sense of security in Him?

PRAY

Heavenly Father, when I feel insecure and question the fairness of life, draw me closer to You. Remind me that true security is found in Your presence and guidance. Help me to trust in Your plan and to seek my refuge in You alone. In Your Son's holy name. Amen.

23. CRUSHED

Oh, How the Mighty Have Fallen

For Sara, you care for us so well, especially when we feel crushed.

Psalm 89

1 I will sing of the steadfast love of the LORD, forever;
with my mouth I will make known Your faithfulness to all generations.
2 For I said, "Steadfast love will be built up forever;
in the heavens You will establish Your faithfulness."
3 You have said, "I have made a covenant with My chosen one;
I have sworn to David My servant:
4 'I will establish Your offspring forever,
and build Your throne for all generations.'" *Selah*

5 Let the heavens praise Your wonders, O LORD,
Your faithfulness in the assembly of the holy ones!
6 For who in the skies can be compared to the LORD?
Who among the heavenly beings is like the LORD,
7 a God greatly to be feared in the council of the holy ones,
and awesome above all who are around him?
8 O LORD God of hosts,
who is mighty as You are, O LORD,
with Your faithfulness all around you?
9 You rule the raging of the sea;
when its waves rise, You still them.
10 You crushed Rahab like a carcass;
You scattered Your enemies with Your mighty arm.

11 The heavens are Yours; the earth also is Yours;
the world and all that is in it, You have founded them.
12 The north and the south, You have created them;
Tabor and Hermon joyously praise Your name.
13 You have a mighty arm;
strong is Your hand, high Your right hand.
14 Righteousness and justice are the foundation of Your throne;
steadfast love and faithfulness go before You.
15 Blessed are the people who know the festal shout,
who walk, O LORD, in the light of Your face,
16 who exult in Your name all the day
and in Your righteousness are exalted.
17 For You are the glory of their strength;
by Your favor our horn is exalted.
18 For our shield belongs to the LORD,
our king to the Holy One of Israel.

19 Of old You spoke in a vision to Your godly one, and said:
"I have granted help to one who is mighty;
I have exalted one chosen from the people.
20 I have found David, My servant;
with My holy oil I have anointed him,
21 so that My hand shall be established with him;
My arm also shall strengthen him.
22 The enemy shall not outwit him;
the wicked shall not humble him.
23 I will crush his foes before him
and strike down those who hate him.
24 My faithfulness and My steadfast love shall be with him,
and in My name shall his horn be exalted.
25 I will set his hand on the sea
and his right hand on the rivers.
26 He shall cry to Me, 'You are my Father,
my God, and the Rock of my salvation.'
27 And I will make him the firstborn,
the highest of the kings of the earth.

28 My steadfast love I will keep for him forever,
and My covenant will stand firm for him.
29 I will establish his offspring forever
and his throne as the days of the heavens.
30 If his children forsake My law
and do not walk according to My rules,
31 if they violate My statutes
and do not keep My commandments,
32 then I will punish their transgression with the rod
and their iniquity with stripes,
33 but I will not remove from him My steadfast love
or be false to My faithfulness.
34 I will not violate My covenant
or alter the word that went forth from My lips.
35 Once for all I have sworn by My holiness;
I will not lie to David.
36 His offspring shall endure forever,
his throne as long as the sun before Me.
37 Like the moon it shall be established forever,
a faithful witness in the skies." *Selah*

38 But now You have cast off and rejected;
You are full of wrath against Your anointed.
39 You have renounced the covenant with Your servant;
You have defiled his crown in the dust.
40 You have breached all his walls;
You have laid his strongholds in ruins.
41 All who pass by plunder him;
he has become the scorn of his neighbors.
42 You have exalted the right hand of his foes;
You have made all his enemies rejoice.
43 You have also turned back the edge of his sword,
and You have not made him stand in battle.
44 You have made his splendor to cease
and cast his throne to the ground.
45 You have cut short the days of his youth;
You have covered him with shame. *Selah*

46 How long, O LORD? Will You hide Yourself forever?
How long will Your wrath burn like fire?
47 Remember how short my time is!
For what vanity You have created all the children of man!
48 What man can live and never see death?
Who can deliver his soul from the power of Sheol? *Selah*

49 Lord, where is Your steadfast love of old,
which by Your faithfulness You swore to David?
50 Remember, O Lord, how Your servants are mocked,
and how I bear in my heart the insults of all the many nations,
51 with which Your enemies mock, O LORD,
with which they mock the footsteps of Your anointed.

52 Blessed be the LORD forever!
Amen and Amen.

Is there anything more pitiful than a once-great person reduced to a humbling, humiliating position?

Think of these scenarios: The star high school quarterback now in a bar twenty years later, still bragging about the state championship. The megachurch pastor after the scandal left him humiliated now joining a new church as a humble nobody. A once beloved and charismatic professor subbing in a middle school class that doesn't listen to her. The mom who used to run the annual gala sitting alone in the corner after her kids have graduated. The once brilliant and respected doctor as a feeble, confused patient in a memory-care unit.

This type of humiliation guts me every single time. You too? We love the stories of God's outrageous blessings. The miraculous healing. The atheist who comes to faith. The tiny church that is packed every Sunday. I could live in this kind mountaintop, constant-blessing Christianity and never need any gritty reality.

We don't like to look at what happens after the happily ever after. Keep your sequel. Leave us with the shiny moment of glory, the long-awaited vows, the Gatorade dumped over the coach, the worst-to-first, end-of-season victory.

Yet, this is how stories actually go. The trajectory of what goes up must come down. No human stays at the top forever. Eventually, our weakness wins out. Eventually, we're crushed.

David knew how it felt to be crushed. His people disappointed him, political enemies tried to kill him, and his own sin sabotaged him. But what he describes in this psalm is something different. This is the gut punch that seems to come from God Himself.

After all, God had ordained David as chosen (see 1 Samuel 16:12–13; 2 Samuel 7:8–9; Psalm 89:19–21). If his success was clearly from God, then what should he make of the fact his sons aren't heirs to the throne? Where is God's blessing now? David—in his anguish—calls out to God for forsaking him.

Then, thousands of years later, Jesus does the same. Jesus had lived a perfect life as true man and true God. He had loved, taught, healed, and cared for the people in God's name. Then came Palm Sunday, with crowds cheering His name. He was at the height of His popularity.

But now, this part is true too. The unfair, unearned conviction. The cross. The torture. The slow, public, humiliating death. Terrible darkness. Excruciating pain. The real hurt of all that would have been startling even to the one who knew it was coming. This is anguish.

Yes, David's reign ends. Yes, Jesus hangs on a cross. But God's plan will unfold. His promises are still eternal and will never fail. Humanity will rise and fall. The earth will crumble. God redeems all of this. His faithfulness endures forever.

As believers, we look to the long view. We know that everything will indeed be crushed. We also trust that God's love will always continue.

And so, you and I believe that because God's faithfulness is revealed throughout the Bible, we can trust that our current suffering is part of that goodness. It's so hard and humiliating, and we could really use a glimmer of the former glory. But, if God isn't giving it right now, then that is part of His epic story. This is so painful in the moment. The feeling of being crushed seems like exactly that—complete destruction of our plans and complete dependence on Him.

I am so sorry. This is hard. There's nothing else for us to do but keep praising His goodness while we wait for the next door to open. I so wish this was not the way the system worked. I wish it was always joy, never-ending goodness, and deep and easy peace. But that's only in heaven.

This is what was on David's mind while he wrote this song and what was on Jesus' mind while He died on the cross. One day, this all will be healed, all will be completed, and all the loose ends will be tied up. One day, we won't walk in shame; we will walk in glory!

And then, we will understand everything.

ABOUT PSALM 89

Psalm 89 captures both the joy of trusting in God and the deep heartache of feeling crushed by the sinful world. The psalmist begins by celebrating God's promises. But as this psalm unfolds, he is crushed by the reality of life.

We've all been exactly here—when it seems like God is far away and life pins us down. Feel that pain and disappointment. Feel the sadness. Feel the chaos of emotions that come when your hopes are crushed.

The Trajectory of the Psalm

Yet, even in the middle of his anguish, David remembers who God is. It's a moment of perspective—life feels overwhelming, but God's power and love haven't changed. David takes the long view.

What makes Psalm 89 so relatable is that it doesn't pretend that everything is okay. There's no quick fix or sudden resolution. David is still wrestling with his pain at the end of the psalm.

But he doesn't let go of God. He doesn't let go of hope. Even when we're crushed, even when the answers don't come right away, God is with us in the struggle.

The Hope of the Anointed One

Jesus knew what it was like to be crushed. On the cross, He bore the weight of the world's pain caused by sin, including yours. But in His resurrection, we see that God's promises always come through. Even when it feels like hope is gone, Jesus' victory over sin and death show us that hope is never gone.

Amen & Amen

Psalm 89 gives us permission to feel crushed, to bring our hurt to God, and to trust that His promises are still true. His love hasn't left, and He's still faithful, working through the pain to bring us to a place of hope. We may not see it yet, but we can trust that joy will come again. We can trust because God says it is so. He is with us, even in the hardest moments.

Blessed be the Lord forever! Amen and amen.

DISCUSS PSALM 89

1. How does Psalm 89 help you process feelings of being crushed or overwhelmed by life's disappointments?

2. In what ways do we find hope in God's faithfulness and promises, even while trudging through life's disappointments?

PRAY

Father, when I feel crushed by life's trials, I come to You seeking comfort and strength. I know that You understand my pain and are a refuge in times of distress. Lift my spirit and renew my hope as I trust in Your everlasting love and promises. Help me to lean on Your strength and find peace in Your presence. In Your Son's name. Amen.

24. UNSURE

You Are the Coolest Camper—Like, Totally Cool

For Nate, you are the coolest.

Psalm 94

1O LORD, God of vengeance,
    O God of vengeance, shine forth!
2Rise up, O judge of the earth;
    repay to the proud what they deserve!
3O LORD, how long shall the wicked,
    how long shall the wicked exult?
4They pour out their arrogant words;
    all the evildoers boast.
5They crush Your people, O LORD,
    and afflict Your heritage.
6They kill the widow and the sojourner,
    and murder the fatherless;
7and they say, "The LORD does not see;
    The God of Jacob does not perceive."

8Understand, O dullest of the people!
    Fools, when will you be wise?
9He who planted the ear, does He not hear?
He who formed the eye, does He not see?
10He who disciplines the nations, does He not rebuke?
He who teaches man knowledge—

11 the LORD—knows the thoughts of man,
 that they are but a breath.
12 Blessed is the man whom You discipline, O LORD,
 and whom You teach out of Your law,
13 to give him rest from days of trouble,
 until a pit is dug for the wicked.
14 For the LORD will not forsake His people;
 He will not abandon His heritage;
15 for justice will return to the righteous,
 and all the upright in heart will follow it.

16 Who rises up for me against the wicked?
 Who stands up for me against evildoers?
17 If the LORD had not been my help,
 my soul would soon have lived in the land of silence.
18 When I thought, "My foot slips,"
 Your steadfast love, O LORD, held me up.
19 When the cares of my heart are many,
 Your consolations cheer my soul.
20 Can wicked rulers be allied with You,
 those who frame injustice by statute?
21 They band together against the life of the righteous
 and condemn the innocent to death.
22 But the LORD has become my stronghold,
 and my God the rock of my refuge.
23 He will bring back on them their iniquity
 and wipe them out for their wickedness;
 the LORD our God will wipe them out.

Our friend Scott writes and directs movies. Our family loves being part of the process.

Nate was especially interested in the films. Scott told him that he should be in one of his movies one day. Nate was a fifth grader at the time and loved the idea. He was still a little kid, still goofy and enchanted by the thought of making people believe he was someone else.

Then, a year and a half later, Scott asked Nate to audition. In the months between, though, Nate had changed. Now he was a middle schooler, played soccer, and was interested in girls. Acting silly to become a character wasn't as appealing. But he was still curious, so when Scott sent the script and told Nate to create an audition video, he agreed.

The movie they would be filming was set at a Christian camp. It was called *Myles from Home,* and it was a fun film with campy (ha!) acting. All the shooting would take place at a summer camp a few hours away from our home.

Nate sent an audition video and landed a pretty good first role—as a camper—partly because the production team appreciated his clear speaking voice and partly because they liked his look. For weeks before the shoot, Nate practiced his five lines until it felt like he could do this.

Then, the day came, and we drove to the camp for a long day of shooting on the last day of production. The week had been bonkers busy, and we hadn't talked much about the shoot. I sensed Nate was scared. As we drove, I talked to him about being a professional. The other actors had been shooting together for a while and had bonded; Nate wouldn't have the same closeness. Still, the crew needed Nate to step in and do his job. He responded with a quiet, "But I don't know what I'm doing." I felt that. I started to worry.

Within a few minutes of being on set, I saw that I was right to worry. The other kids playing campers were real actors, like the kind that had agents and managers and were really into warming up with vocal exercises. They were shouting and laughing and acting out scenes from cartoons. They were the kind of kids who had zero self-consciousness. Nate was all self-consciousness. I looked at him and said, "For just one day, you have to be an actor."

Everyone was invested in this new kid figuring out this acting thing fast. Because of budget and schedule headaches, the crew needed Nate to transform himself into a character who was comfortable being melodramatic—and not at all like the cynical teenage soccer player he played in real life.

As we began to film, Nate's tension was all over his face. His anxiety came through in every line he delivered. During breaks, the other actors suggested he loosen up a bit. I watched as Nate learned how hard acting is and how high the stakes are when you have to make magic happen in one day.

Throughout the morning, the assistant director, Kenda, kept pulling Nate out for a "quick talk." She pushed him to deliver his lines with more passion and less of the slightly sarcastic tone he'd developed. The other parents on set started giving him pointers too. Was this nonactor going to ruin their kids' hard work? Nate was getting tired of all the corrections and promised he would say his lines any way they wanted.

But he just couldn't do it. When we broke for lunch, Nate took one look at the other kids together at the picnic table and veered to eat with me. As soon as he sat down, he started talking, "I can't act like that. It's not me. Can we just leave? Someone else can do this better."

We tried praying. I reminded Nate to relax and let God work through him. Scott sat with us and gave Nate acting tips. But the anxiety from all the pressure was wearing him out. It had already been a long day, and we still had to shoot the big campfire scene, the climax of the movie.

By the time the whole crew gathered for this big night scene, it was very late. We were all punchy and irritable from the stressful day. And still, every line Nate said took dozens of takes. Then, the production crew would watch the footage, huddle up, look over at Nate, ask him to use more passion, and shoot it again. I had tears in my eyes, and I could see the same exhaustion in Nate's face.

Eventually, Kenda had an epiphany. She pulled Nate aside and brought me over to a little grove of trees near the campfire. She put her hands on his shoulders and said, "Here's what we're going to do. You're going to be the coolest kid in camp. You get that? Say your lines loud, but don't act like a goofy camper. Instead, act like a skeptical one. You are so much better than all these other campers. You are literally the coolest kid ever. Can you do that?"

Nate grinned. "I can do that." The uncertainty that had been on his face since the minute we got there disappeared, and he put his whole self into being the coolest kid in camp.

It worked—pretty well. Or, at least well enough for us to finish the scene and the long day of shooting. We gathered our stuff, hugged the production team, and thanked everyone for the experience.

On the way home, Nate and I talked about the day, especially about his uncertainty. Now, in the safety of the dark car, he could finally share how excruciating it had been. He had not liked it at all—feeling so unsure, letting the team down, knowing he couldn't do what they wanted. Later, when the film came out, Nate watched it one time, cringing with embarrassment, and never watched it again.

So much of life is like this. Sometimes you really just don't know. You want desperately to move forward but you don't know how. You feel ashamed, dumb, angry, and anxious. This is part of what David was writing about in Psalm 94. We are unsure, and God is right there to help us. He fights for us. He comforts us. We listen for the next steps and hope God will provide a way.

What about you? Maybe you're not stuck on a movie set, trying to figure out how to act. But maybe you're trying to figure out if your current job still suits you. Or you're asking God His plan for you when it seems you're facing a brick wall. Maybe you aren't sure how to deal with a complicated relationship or how to handle a toxic team at work.

When you're unsure, God is sure. Every time. You don't know how to be in this new role. You feel like you are faking it, but He is right there with you. As much as it feels as if you're completely lost, you're not. You are safe. You are secure. You've got this because your heavenly Father has a plan for you. He is with you, listening to your prayers, giving help, and loving you through it all.

Your heavenly Father has a plan for you. And in Christ, that plan is already fulfilled—our salvation is sure, our identity is secure. Even when life feels uncertain, we can trust that Jesus has already gone before us, holding us close.

ABOUT PSALM 94

Psalm 94 is for those times when there are a lot of hard things going on. During a time of political uncertainty, the psalmist called out to God to step in and make things right. The author is begging God to make a way when it seems like there isn't one. Throughout the prayer, we can feel the frustration and fear we still feel today.

Shine On, God

The psalmist begins his prayer by crying out for justice: "O LORD, God of vengeance, O God of vengeance, shine forth!" (v. 1). In the middle of this political wilderness, the psalmist begs God to show the way forward against the enemies.

Shaky Steps

The most relatable image the psalmist paints is in verse 18: "When I thought, 'My foot slips,' Your steadfast love, O LORD, held me up." You know this feeling, the sensation of your foot slipping as you step forward. Then the psalm reminds you that even when you feel like you're slipping, God's love is steady.

Cheer My Soul, Lord

That shaky feeling of uncertainty is part of being human. This is a timeless problem—and so is God's guidance. Read these words in verse 19: "When the cares of my heart are many, Your consolations cheer my soul."

Refuge & Rock

In the unsure season, the psalmist points us to God: "But the LORD has become my stronghold, and my God the rock of my refuge" (v. 22). God is our safe place—our rock—when everything feels like it's shifting.

Identity in Christ

Jesus came to bring peace. By His death and resurrection, God showed us that, even in the chaos, He is sovereign. Jesus is a secure place to rest. By His work, with the Holy Spirit for us, we can know that God's love is always with us.

DISCUSS PSALM 94

1. Read Psalm 94 again. When have you felt your foot slipping lately? How has God provided or how are you asking God to provide?

2. What are some practical ways you can remember God's promises to always take care of you?

PRAY

Lord, You control everything. When I'm afraid and unsure about who I am, remind me that I belong to You. Help me to find my refuge in You. Remind me of Your everlasting peace that I have through Your Holy Spirit. Fill my heart with Your Word as I navigate through this uncertain life, knowing that You are always with me. Amen.

25. GRATEFUL

And Now, We Sing

For Janine, who lives out Psalm 95.

Psalm 95

1 Oh come, let us sing to the LORD;
let us make a joyful noise to the rock of our salvation!
2 Let us come into His presence with thanksgiving;
let us make a joyful noise to Him with songs of praise!
3 For the LORD is a great God,
and a great King above all gods.
4 In His hand are the depths of the earth;
the heights of the mountains are His also.
5 The sea is His, for He made it,
And His hands formed the dry land.

6 Oh come, let us worship and bow down;
let us kneel before the LORD, our Maker!
7 For He is our God,
and we are the people of His pasture,
and the sheep of His hand.
Today, if you hear His voice,
8 do not harden your hearts, as at Meribah,
as on the day at Massah in the wilderness,
9 when your fathers put Me to the test
and put Me to the proof, though they had seen My work.

10 For forty years I loathed that generation
and said, "They are a people who go astray in their heart,
and they have not known My ways."
11 Therefore I swore in My wrath,
"They shall not enter My rest."

Where are we with thank-you notes?

I grew up hating them. Maybe it was because I would one day become a writer and liked filling notebooks with truthful feelings. Obligatory notes felt insincere.

For the next couple decades of wedding gifts and baby showers, I got good at the thank-you note format. Really, they became a formula—a sentence or two exclaiming how I loved the gift, another one praising the giver's generosity/thoughtfulness/wisdom, and a couple of personal thoughts before a closing. Then, the address and the stamp. Signed, sealed, and done.

When my kids were old enough to write more than their names, the great TYN wars started in the Hergenrader house. If I disliked writing them in the snail-mail era, you can imagine how Gen Z (and now Gen Alpha) feels about the whole tradition. Talking on the phone feels archaic to them, let alone putting a stamp on an envelope to thank a friend four streets over for the digital gift card. Thank-you note writing in our house became cruel and unusual punishment.

Having our kids write thank-you notes meant listening to their constant complaining, fixing the envelopes they always incorrectly addressed, and tracking down stamps.

Our youngest son, Nate, thought he had won the TYN war when he declared he would stop having birthday parties if it meant he would never have to write another one of these again. This was right around the same time I found a stash of unsent notes stuffed in the drawer of another kid.

I relented and agreed they could send thank-you texts. Maybe this would make us all feel better about giving thanks where thanks are due? Nope. Thank-you texts are meaningless. We already text, snap, DM, and post all day long. What's one more bit of data in the monsoon of words? Nothing.

In fact, that's exactly where our society as a whole seems to be on thank-you notes.

This month I've attended a couple of baby showers and a wedding. I have received no thank-you notes. I'm sure this is due to the same reason our kids stopped the practice. It's inconvenient and archaic and meaningless.

Except, it's totally not.

When we pause to thank someone for their kindness or effort, it changes our perspective. It helps us appreciate the gift. Not to overstate it, but gratitude helps us appreciate our lives. Every bit of them. Thank-you texts are practically worthless because they don't take much time or much effort. And we pay attention to whatever we do that takes both time and effort.

This is what Psalm 95 does for us. This is the pause to raise a joyful noise, to kneel before the Lord, to hear His voice and not harden our hearts or feel entitled to His gifts.

And so, in the spirit of this thank-you practice, let's follow David's lead and thank God for some of what He has given us. Let's make a joyful noise for everything that brings us joy.

Thank You, God, for no car accidents today. Thank You for every time I laughed this week. Thanks for those who love me and for those I love. Thanks for the million details and blessings in every second of this day, this week, this life.

My family, my pets, this weather, my memories, kind people who help me and I don't even know it, my favorite foods and flavors, that I know more today than I did yesterday, the moments and blessings and love and relationships that I haven't yet experienced but that You have waiting for me. Lord, thank You!

What about you? What are you thankful for? Here's some of what your list might include:

A good night's sleep without interruptions, restored relationships with family members, forgiveness of your sins, presence of the Holy Spirit, sunrises and sunsets that reflect God's glory.

Supportive parents or in-laws, an email that reads "meeting canceled," God's constant love and grace, the ability to serve with a Christlike heart, an unexpected "I love you" from a teenager, God's patience in seasons of doubt.

Healing from illness, clean countertops, Jesus as our cornerstone and rock of salvation, heated seats on cold mornings, learning to trust God more fully, friends who offer encouragement and accountability in faith, continued health and safety of loved ones, strength from the Holy Spirit.

Discovering God's calling in midlife and again in retirement, witnessing answered prayers, soft pajamas at the end of a long day, understanding God's Word more deeply, long dinners with family, knowing Christ is our Good Shepherd, a new episode of your favorite podcast.

God's care for the details of creation, a supportive community of fellow believers, hearing kids laugh together, finding that important document right when you need it, conversations about faith, peace that surpasses understanding, the promise of eternal rest in Christ.

Praise and singing? Yes. Joyful noises to thank God for His gifts? Yes! More of this. Everyone, now!

Because when we all sing praise to God together, it encourages those who are struggling, weary, and not feeling thankful right now. We know this because we've been in the hard, rough place of being disappointed in everything, those dark moments when we feel only sadness. We have felt left out and felt mad at ourselves, at God, and at everyone.

And then . . . someone reflects light and you see their real joy about life. Someone helps you remember that—oh, yeah!—there is so much good still happening here. Someone reminds you that, even in our darkest times, even if the problems aren't resolved the way we want them to be, Jesus is still Lord. Jesus is still our Savior.

Let's come before Him with thanksgiving. Because when we praise Him, our perspective changes. Not because of anything we have done to make it happen but because His Holy Spirit changes us.

Praise God!

ABOUT PSALM 95

Psalm 95 invites us into a mindset of gratitude that's deep, joyful, and real. It opens with such an energetic call: "Oh come, let us sing to the LORD; let us make a joyful noise to the rock of our salvation!" (v. 1). There is no holding back here; this is gratitude that overflows into praise. This verse is an expression of being so aware of who God is and what He's done that we can't help but respond with thankfulness. This is the kind of gratitude that fills you up and spills over into every part of your life.

Powerful & Personal

Psalm 95 calls us to be grateful as it reminds us how powerful God is. "For the LORD is a great God, and a great King above all gods" (v. 3). Stop and reflect how incredible it is that the Creator of the universe cares about us personally. His hands shaped the mountains, the seas, and every part of creation (vv. 4–5). At the same time, He is intimately involved in the details of our lives. Gratitude flows from remembering that God is both vast and close, holding the world together while also holding each of us.

Not only does God take care of us but we see our own weakness when we see Him. "Oh come, let us worship and bow down; let us kneel before the LORD, our Maker! For He is our God, and we are the people of His pasture, and the sheep of His hand" (vv. 6–7). God guides us, cares for us, and watches over us. God's people read this to prepare to worship Him. How appropriate to recognize our tendency to lose our way—and the joy when God brings us back.

Choose Joy

This is also a call to not let our hearts harden. The psalmist warns us not to turn away like the Israelites did in the wilderness when they forgot God's goodness (vv. 8–11). Psalm 95 reminds us that gratitude is a way of staying soft toward God and of keeping our hearts open to His presence and work in our lives. It's a way of remembering His faithfulness, even when we're going through tough times. When we hold on to gratitude, it helps us trust God more deeply and keeps our hearts in tune with His voice.

Jesus: Our King, Our Rest

Psalm 95 points to Jesus as the King worthy of worship and the one who provides true rest. This is our gratitude—through Christ's sacrifice, we have a love that never ends, a grace that covers every failure, and a rest that is secure in Him.

In Jesus, every reason for thanksgiving finds its fulfillment.

DISCUSS PSALM 95

1. List what you're thankful for in this very moment. Start small, with the blessings right in front of you, and keep listing everything you can think of for two minutes.

2. How can you encourage others to share their thankfulness and praise to God like in the example we see in Psalm 95?

PRAY

Father, King, Lord, thank You for everything in my day. You have perfect plans for me and provide exactly what I need in every hour and every detail of my life. Change my perspective so I can praise You even in my struggles. Most of all, dear God, thank You for Your Son, Jesus. In His name. Amen.

Conclusion

Goodbye for now, dear reader.

Thank you for joining me on this journey through Psalms.

As we walked through these ancient songs together, I hope you didn't just read the words—I hope you *felt* them.

The Psalms capture the real ups and downs of life: the big joys, the deep hurts, and the raw, honest cries to God. You've experienced that alongside me, and I'm so grateful.

As a coach, I've learned that real growth comes when we stay in our emotions long enough to understand them. It's not about rushing to fix things. It's about letting ourselves *be* in those feelings—whether fear, sadness, or frustration—and trusting that God will work through it. David and the psalmists understood this, and we read the Psalms because in them is a lesson that still matters today.

We've seen how these words, written so long ago, still speak to us today. They remind us that God's love is steady even when life feels out of control. We're part of a bigger family of believers who've held on to these promises, cried out to God for help, and celebrated His goodness. That's pretty amazing.

So, as you finish this book, here's what I hope you take with you: God is right here with you. His love doesn't change. His grace is always enough. And He's closer than you think.

Thank you for giving the Psalms a place in your heart. Thank you for letting them shape your prayers and speak to your life. And most of all, thank you for leaning into God's love, a love that has carried people through every struggle and will keep carrying you through every moment of this life until you see Him face to face.

May these psalms stay with you, even after this book is closed.

With love and prayers,
Christina Hergenrader

P.S. Let's keep in touch! I would love to hear from you. Connect with me at christina@christinasbooks.com and tell me your story of God's grace. Or just say hi.

More Psalms & Emotions

1. When you feel *terrified*: Psalm 91

   "He will cover you with His pinions, and under His wings you will find refuge" (v. 4).

2. When you feel *sad*: Psalm 42

   "Why are you cast down, O my soul, and why are you in turmoil within me? Hope in God" (v. 5).

3. When you feel *relieved*: Psalm 103

   "Bless the LORD, O my soul, and forget not all His benefits" (v. 2).

4. When you feel *scattered*: Psalm 46

   "Be still, and know that I am God" (v. 10).

5. When you feel *heartbroken*: Psalm 147

   "He heals the brokenhearted and binds up their wounds" (v. 3).

6. When you feel *glad*: Psalm 92

   "It is good to give thanks to the LORD, to sing praises to Your name, O Most High" (v. 1).

7. When you feel *regretful*: Psalm 38

   "For my iniquities have gone over my head; like a heavy burden, they are too heavy for me" (v. 4).

8. When you feel *ashamed*: Psalm 51

   "Have mercy on me, O God, according to Your steadfast love; according to Your abundant mercy blot out my transgressions" (v. 1).

9. When you feel *oppressed*: Psalm 9

   "The LORD is a stronghold for the oppressed, a stronghold in times of trouble" (v. 9).

10. When you feel *angry*: Psalm 140

"Deliver me, O LORD, from evil men; preserve me from violent men" (v. 1).

11. When you feel *guilty*: Psalm 32

"Blessed is the one whose transgression is forgiven, whose sin is covered" (v. 1).

12. When you feel *insecure*: Psalm 130

"I wait for the LORD, my soul waits, and in His word I hope" (v. 5).

13. When you feel *wonder*; Psalm 8

"When I look at Your heavens, the work of Your fingers, the moon and the stars, which You have set in place" (v. 3).

14. When you feel *peaceful*: Psalm 62

"For God alone my soul waits in silence; from Him comes my salvation" (v. 1).

15. When you feel *thankful*: Psalm 145

"The LORD is gracious and merciful, slow to anger and abounding in steadfast love" (v. 8).

16. When you feel *uncertain*: Psalm 86

"Teach me Your way, O LORD, that I may walk in Your truth" (v. 11).

17. When you feel *isolated*: Psalm 142

"Look to the right and see: there is none who takes notice of me" (v. 4).

18. When you feel *exuberant*: Psalm 150

"Let everything that has breath praise the LORD! Praise the LORD!" (v. 6).

19. When you feel *inspired*: Psalm 19

"The heavens declare the glory of God, and the sky above proclaims His handiwork" (v. 1).

20. When you feel God's *faithfulness*: Psalm 66

"Come and see what God has done: He is awesome in His deeds toward the children of man" (v. 5).

Acknowledgments

Mike: Thanks for all the hours in, conversations about, and support for this book. Every book is for you. Perhaps this one most of all.

Catie: Your energetic, passionate faith inspires so many people—including me.

Sam: You're all over these pages. May you always know God is with you.

Elisabeth: Thanks for showing me how to get stuff done. You never stop.

Nate: Your curiosity and enthusiasm are a model for me and for the world.

Mom and Dad: You have researched, read countless drafts, and prayed so fervently for this book. I really don't know what I would do without both of you.

Mark and Marcilee: Your daily support means everything. Thank you for showing up.

Jen and Kenny: Let's make this our best decade yet. Love you both!

Melissa and Connie: You're my soul sisters, and I love you more every year.

Theresa and Janine: Thanks for parenting with me through the peaks and valleys.

My AYF Students: I love each and every one of you. And not just because you listened to this book every class period. (Although that was really nice.)

The women of LWML: Thank you for all your encouragement and support.

Dr. Chen: Thank you for your wisdom and kindness.

Sara: Thanks for hosting Bible study while I talked A LOT about these exact thoughts.

Michelle Diercks and Deb Burma: You will never know how much your encouragement has meant to me.

Aunt Katie: You have prayed me through every season. I'm beyond grateful for every single one of your one million prayers.

Everyone who prayed for this book: Thank you. I felt the power of your prayers and I am forever grateful for them.

Elizabeth and Erica: You make my books come alive, and I love doing this with you. Thanks for being so good at all of it and working tirelessly to spread God's Word.

Peggy: May our work together continue to endure.

Laura: Another project! Thanks for your support and quick thinking to make this happen.

God: All the words of Psalm 40, for You, my Lord and Savior.